"Spinster, of No Occupation" ?

Mary Ellen Shaw 1859-1926

by Rowena Edlin-White

smallprint

Published by *smallprint* 2007
an imprint of *Woolgatherings*,
11 Frederick Ave, Carlton, Nottingham NG4 1HP
England, UK

ISBN 978-1-900074-21-6

Printed by Fineprint, Nottingham NG3 2NJ

Contents

Illustrations

Engraving opp. page 1 from *In and About Nottinghamshire* by Mellors, 1908
All photographs in centre pages except No. 5 property of Myra Chilvers
No. 11 used by permission of the Methodist Studies Unit, Oxford Brookes University
All other illustrations property of the author

Owthorpe Hall, Owthorpe, Nottinghamshire
(now demolished)

Preface

When Mary Ellen Shaw died on 24th December 1926, her death certificate, issued the same day, was filled out meticulously. It tells us that her home was 86 Mansfield Road, that she was the daughter of John Shaw, Registrar of Births and Deaths, deceased; it tells in detail the cause of death. But one thing it doesn't tell: in the column headed 'Rank or Profession' it states, erroneously, "Spinster of no occupation".

Nothing could have been further from the truth. Mary Ellen Shaw had worked unceasingly from her early teens in paid employment as a daily governess of small children, as a music teacher and as an unpaid social worker in the poorer areas of Nottingham, especially in St Ann's and Sneinton. Early work in the Sunday Schools attached to the Wesleyan Chapel on Mansfield Road extended to visiting pupils in their homes and delivering tracts locally. Workhouse, prison and hospital visiting followed and developed with time into organising Evening Homes and holidays for factory girls; convalescent accommodation for poor women; adoptions for the illegitimate babies of "her" girls; a Babies Guild to teach parenting skills to women in deprived areas; and finally, in 1901, her most inspirational and successful venture — "Miss Shaw's Men's Bible Class" — which, with the financial backing of the Duchess of Portland, offered moral support to huge numbers of working men (and women) in Nottingham and Mansfield.

Mary Ellen Shaw was unflagging in her devotion to all these different causes and initiatives in the city of Nottingham. She became expert at gathering funds from her wealthier friends and associates to answer the many cries for help she heard and tried to answer, but much of the burden was taken upon her own shoulders and she died in harness. As the daughter and sister-in-law of registrars she would have been aware of the conventions in filling out death certificates, but to record for posterity that she had "no occupation" does her a grave injustice.

This book aims to set the record straight. It has been a great privilege to do so with the support and encouragement of Mary Ellen's great-niece, Myra Chilvers, who first lured me into the project with the wealth of diaries, photographs and documents which have survived to tell the tale of Mary Ellen Shaw, a woman of whom Nottingham should be proud.

Rowena Edlin-White, October 2007

I would also like to acknowledge the help and interest of:

Dee Duke
Rob Edlin-White
Derek Adlam, Curator, the Welbeck Estate
The Bromley Library
Peter Forsaith, Methodist Studies Unit, The Wesley Centre, Oxford
Hucknall Library
Nerissa Mcdonald, Brackenhurst College
Newark Cemetery
Newark Local History Library
Nottingham Local History Library
Nottinghamshire Archives
Southwell Minster Library
Wilford Historical Society

RENSHAWS

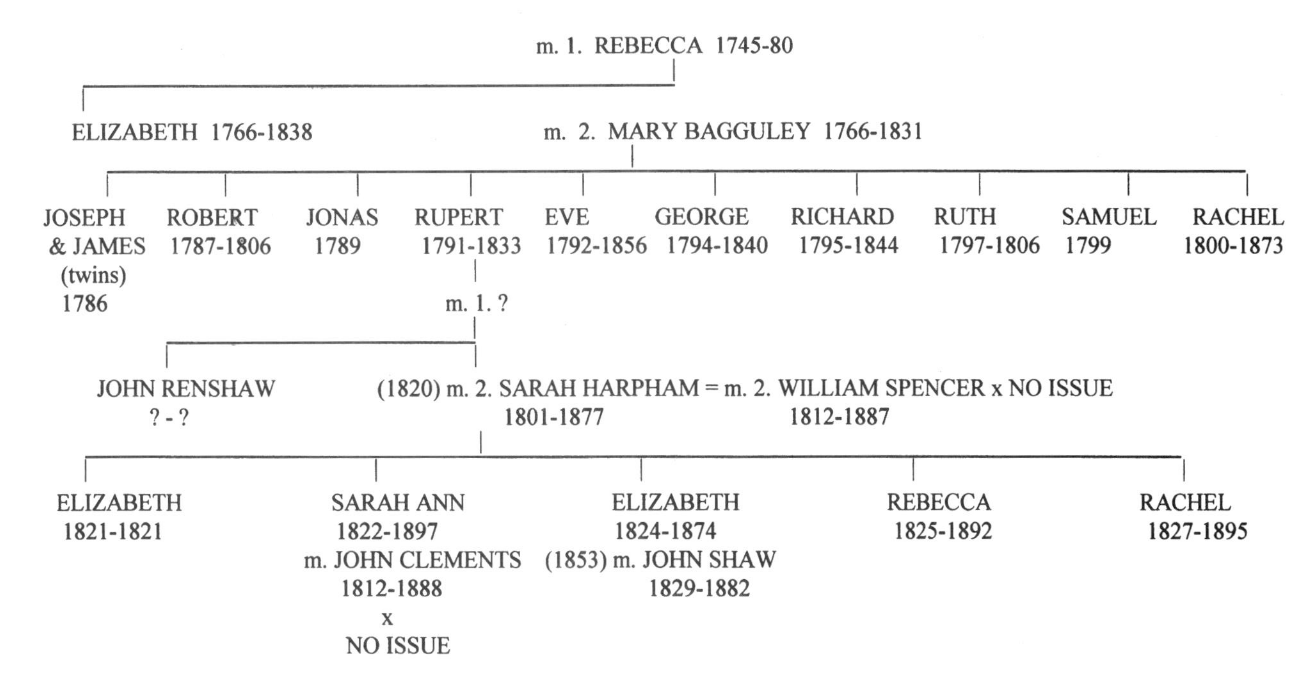
JOHN RENSHAW OF OWTHORPE 1742-1802
m. 1. REBECCA 1745-80
ELIZABETH 1766-1838
m. 2. MARY BAGGULEY 1766-1831
JOSEPH & JAMES (twins) 1786
ROBERT 1787-1806
JONAS 1789
RUPERT 1791-1833
EVE 1792-1856
GEORGE 1794-1840
RICHARD 1795-1844
RUTH 1797-1806
SAMUEL 1799
RACHEL 1800-1873
m. 1. ?
JOHN RENSHAW ? - ?
(1820) m. 2. SARAH HARPHAM = m. 2. WILLIAM SPENCER x NO ISSUE
1801-1877
1812-1887
ELIZABETH 1821-1821
SARAH ANN 1822-1897
m. JOHN CLEMENTS 1812-1888
x
NO ISSUE
ELIZABETH 1824-1874
(1853) m. JOHN SHAW 1829-1882
REBECCA 1825-1892
RACHEL 1827-1895

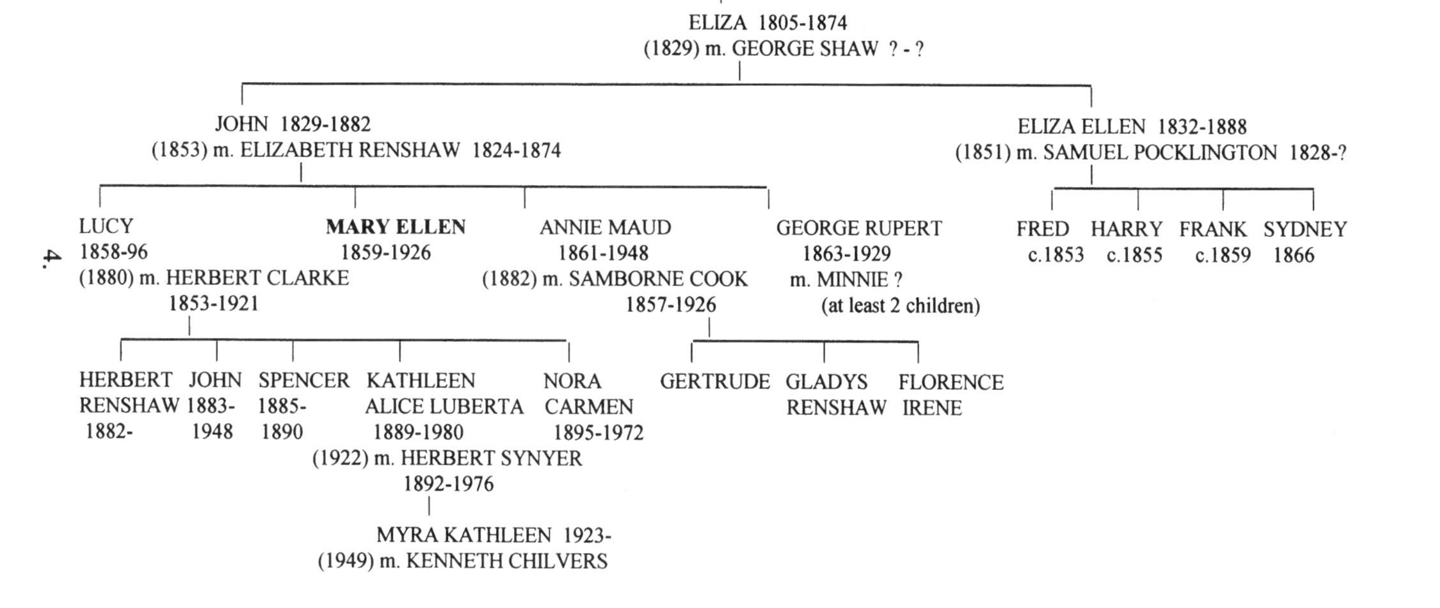
SHAWS
JOHN & ELLEN DOLEMAN
c.1783? c.1785?
ELIZA 1805-1874
(1829) m. GEORGE SHAW ? - ?
JOHN 1829-1882
(1853) m. ELIZABETH RENSHAW 1824-1874
ELIZA ELLEN 1832-1888
(1851) m. SAMUEL POCKLINGTON 1828-?
LUCY
1858-96
(1880) m. HERBERT CLARKE
1853-1921
MARY ELLEN
1859-1926
ANNIE MAUD
1861-1948
(1882) m. SAMBORNE COOK
1857-1926
GEORGE RUPERT
1863-1929
m. MINNIE ?
(at least 2 children)
FRED
c.1853
HARRY
c.1855
FRANK
c.1859
SYDNEY
1866
HERBERT
RENSHAW
1882-
JOHN
1883-
1948
SPENCER
1885-
1890
KATHLEEN
ALICE LUBERTA
1889-1980
(1922) m. HERBERT SYNYER
1892-1976
NORA
CARMEN
1895-1972
GERTRUDE
GLADYS
RENSHAW
FLORENCE
IRENE
MYRA KATHLEEN 1923-
(1949) m. KENNETH CHILVERS

Chapter 1: The Early Years

Mary Ellen Shaw was born on 1st October 1859 in Smithy Row, Nottingham. Her father, John Shaw, was a master jeweller and her mother Elizabeth was, by birth, a Renshaw. Mary Ellen was their second child; her elder sister Lucy had been born in 1858 and Annie Maud and George Rupert were to follow in 1861 and 1863 respectively. The Shaws and the Renshaws were to have an enduring influence on Mary Ellen, so we will briefly examine their background.

The Shaws

John Shaw was the son of George Shaw, a currier[1] and his wife Eliza née Doleman. George and Eliza lived in Bridlesmith Gate and were married in St Peter's Church, Nottingham on 25th July 1829. John's birth followed a very few months later and he was duly baptised in St Peter's on 6th December. His sister Eliza Ellen was also baptised there on 24th June 1832. Little is known of the origins of George Shaw, but the Dolemans were well established in the parish; originally from West Bromwich, John Doleman was a jeweller and silversmith in Nottingham from the 1820s. His daughter Eliza was born in Birmingham, so he may also have been involved in the jewellery trade in that city.

The young Shaw family were to be found living in Newark in 1841, where they remained. We lose trace of George after this, but Eliza Shaw was appointed Librarian of the Mechanics Institute in Newark in the early 1840s. Records state that she held this position in 1844 and that she was still in her post in 1864, some twenty years later. On the 1851 census, her daughter Eliza Ellen was also employed there as assistant Librarian, and John Shaw, aged twenty-one, was a journeyman jeweller working for his grandfather John Doleman at 2 Smithy Row, Nottingham, with whom it is reasonable to suppose he served his apprenticeship. Eliza Ellen married

---

1 A currier was a dresser and dyer of leather, often making bridles and other tackle for horses.

Samuel Pocklington, son of Thomas Pocklington, a publican, in Newark later that same year.

The Renshaws

The origins of the Renshaw family are to be found in the village of Owthorpe. John Renshaw (1742-1802) became the tenant of Owthorpe Hall in 1773 and land agent for the owner, Sir George Smith Bromley of East Stoke. It was occupied by the Renshaw family until 1825 when John's daughter Elizabeth was evicted by Sir George's heir. There are several elegant Renshaw memorials to be seen in the parish church of St Margaret. Rupert Renshaw was the fifth of eleven children born to John Renshaw and his second wife, Mary Bagguley, in 1791. He married Sarah Harpham, a farmer's daughter of Wilford on 9th November 1820 at St Wilfrid's Church. He is recorded as being a bachelor, except that he wasn't; he had been married before, or, at least, he already had a son, John. Rupert, a lace manufacturer and latterly victualler of the Albion Hotel[2], Sherwin Road, New Lenton, had five children with Sarah of whom four survived: Sarah Ann, born 1822, Elizabeth in 1824, Rebecca in 1825 and Rachel 1827. These four were to become Mary Ellen's mother and aunts. Rupert died in 1833, aged just forty-two, and is buried at Wilford.

We can only speculate about his financial circumstances, but what is certain is that Rupert Renshaw's widow and daughters were obliged to work for their livings. For some years the eldest and youngest girls, Sarah Ann and Rachel were cared for by their grandparents, William and Ann Harpham, on the farm at Wilford, while Sarah Renshaw and her two middle daughters are to be found in 1841 working in Bromley Place, Nottingham — she and Rebecca as dressmakers and Elizabeth as a straw hat maker. In 1844 they had their own business in Chapel Bar.

Sarah Renshaw married again, in 1849[3], to William Spencer, a lace manufacturer, the person Mary Ellen and her siblings knew as their Grandpa Spencer. They were still living at Bromley Place on the 1851 census, but moved to Wilford some time in the next ten years, probably on the death of

---

2 Demolished 1972.

3 They were married at St Nicholas' Church on 15th March 1849.

Sarah's father, William Harpham, in 1852. Leastwise, by 1861 William Spencer had exchanged lace manufacture for farming.

Sarah Spencer's daughter, Elizabeth Renshaw, married John Shaw at St Mary's Church, Nottingham on 6th September 1853. He was a bachelor of twenty-four, a jeweller of Smithy Row and she a spinster of twenty-nine, living in Goldsmith Street. Her father, Rupert Renshaw, is noted as deceased, but John's father, George Shaw is not, although a definite date and place for his demise has yet to be discovered. The marriage was witnessed by Elizabeth's step-father William Spencer and her brother John Renshaw. Elizabeth and John Shaw lived at 14 Bromley Place for a while but they had moved in at Smithy Row by the time their first child, Lucy, was born in 1858. Here too Mary Ellen was born the following year, followed by Annie Maud in 1861 and George Rupert in 1863.

All this time, John Shaw worked in the jewellery trade at various premises. At census time in 1861 he was at 5 Long Row East, then moved to 12 Clumber Street and later to 32 Goldsmith Street. Then, he suddenly made a complete change of career. In 1874 he appears in the trade directories as Registrar of Births and Deaths for St Ann's Ward at 24 Milton Street. Later that year, the family settled for good at 26 Mansfield Road[4], a large, solid terraced house just above Woodborough Road.

Registrars

John Shaw "lived over the shop", as it were; a Registrar was obliged to live in his particular district and John's office was at the end of the yard. The job was not properly salaried until the 1920s, but paid according to the number of registrations. People would come to him to register births and deaths or he might have to visit them in their homes — a risky business in the packed lanes and yards of the city centre, when disease was rife. After 1875, he was paid 1/- for each visit. The Registrar was answerable to the Registrar General and had to send in quarterly returns and the business of copying out the returns was a constant element in Mary Ellen's life as all the family

---

[4] The number changed over the years as the bottom end of Mansfield Rd. was redeveloped. It was No. 12 by the 1881 census and by 1901 it was No. 86.

pitched in to get them done on time. It was a tedious business and she used to write them standing up — to keep from falling asleep on the job.

It is not known where Mary Ellen and her siblings were educated but by the age of sixteen she was employed as a teacher herself. Three youthful diaries survive, kept from 1st October 1875 (her sixteenth birthday) until August 26th 1877 when she was nearly eighteen, which tell a great deal about the home life, employment and chapel life of the Shaw family:

> **Oct. 1 1875**: It is my birthday today and I have decided to keep a diary for I think it would be very interesting as well as good for me to do so. I am today 16 years but I have no desire to be any older, and I am governess at Captain Holden's, at Bramcot (sic) to teach their two little boys aged 7 and nine in plain English and so far I like it very much. Mamma is dead but I cannot enter into the particulars of her death as they would seem too painful to do so and it is my intention in writing this diary just to simply state how my time passes in every day life. And now to commence this diary. I got up on this Friday morning feeling a sense of pleasure in thinking what day it was. Maude[5] did my hair for I wear it up and cannot do it myself. We had breakfast and I told Pappa it was my birthday he kissed me and wished very happy returns - so they all did. I went in the morning to Bramcot and in the afternoon Grandma Shaw came and we had tea. I afterwards went to cut the grass at the Cemetery on dear Ma's grave but as it was getting late had not time to finish it so came home. Talked to Grandma and went to Prayer Meeting at half past 7 with Maude. It was conducted by Rev. T. G. Hartley, very few there. Walked up afterward with Mrs Boyns and her daughter. She seemed very nice and we had a very nice talk about Ma, came home, stitched corset bones and after supper George came in and he gave me a watch which pleased me and surprized me very much, he had not been wearing it for some time and it wanted regulating so I am going to take it to Mr Perry to have it set right again. Went to bed and prayed earnestly for help to love God more and more and to be more devoted to him & his service.

Elizabeth Shaw had died suddenly in the early hours of Christmas Day 1874, an event which shocked and distressed her children, especially Mary Ellen. She says she cannot bear to write about it, but at the very end of the first diary, she does finally bring herself to record her mother's death in painful detail. She was buried in the Rock Cemetery on Mansfield Road and

---

5 The spelling of Maud's name is not consistent either in the diaries or in official listings. It will normally be rendered as Maud without the 'e'.

Mary Ellen would often go there when she had a moment, to tidy the grave. She obviously missed her dreadfully. After their mother's death, the children were left somewhat to fend for themselves. Lucy, aged sixteen, seems to have assumed her mother's role — not so far as running the home was concerned, but in accompanying her father to formal dinners and social occasions. Maud, or Madge, as she was also known, was only thirteen and George eleven. Although they had a live-in servant, the girls were supposed to take turns with the housekeeping, something which Lucy seems to have largely avoided and Mary Ellen did not find easy. The daily tasks were added to by a succession of temporary lodgers — lay ministers attached to the Wesleyan chapels and family acquaintances from Newark.

The Shaws did receive practical and moral support from both sides of the family: Grandma Shaw now lived in the household of her son-in-law, Sam Pocklington, chief clerk for maltsters Gilstrap and Sons, at Trent House[6] in Newark. She travelled tirelessly back and forth, often living with her son's family in Nottingham for weeks at a time. She tried to teach Mary Ellen the basics of cooking and housekeeping, though it was something of a uphill struggle. "Aunt Pocklington" (Eliza Ellen) often visited, too, and stayed over with her children Fred, Frank, Harry and Sydney. Then they would have fun playing charades or putting on impromptu concerts.

On the other side, the Spencers, their unmarried daughters Rachel and Rebecca Renshaw and married daughter Sarah Ann Clements, were always ready to welcome the family at Wilford. Sadly, Grandma Spencer died in 1877, but the farm[7] remained a precious refuge for Mary Ellen until it was finally sold in 1896.

Apart from family, a near neighbour, Mrs Fisher, also "kept an eye" on them when their father and grandmother were absent. Describing her mother's death, Mary Ellen remarks, "Mrs Fisher's kindness can never be forgotten, she it was who lifted Ma into the coffin and helped and advised

---

[6] Trent House was off North Gate, behind Spital Row. This area has since been redeveloped and the exact location is unknown.

[7] It is thought that this was originally the Harpham family farm, demolished when Clifton Bridge was built in the 1950s. It was close enough to the River Trent for the ground floor to be completely submerged during the flooding of October 1875, as Mary Ellen recorded in her diary.

the motherless ones at home, indeed in everything she was most kind and a very great blessing."

At the beginning of her diary of 1875, Mary Ellen has recently begun working for Captain Henry Holden, the Chief Constable of Nottinghamshire, at The Grove, Bramcote. She is teaching "plain English" to his two little boys, (Wil)Fred and Frank, and travelling to Bramcote by train every morning and walking across the fields. She must have only recently finished her own education (there is no evidence that she received any formal teacher training) and has been suddenly precipitated into adulthood — she mentions that she needs help from Maud to put her hair up; in happier circumstances, her girlhood might have been somewhat prolonged. In addition to her regular employment with the Holdens, from 1877 she mentions also going each day to teach at Rylands. This was a mission school begun by the Misses Anne and Mary Barker who ran an "establishment for young ladies" in Broadgate, Beeston.[8] From here Mary Ellen would return home in the afternoon to throw herself into various social endeavours.

The Shaws attended the Wesley Chapel on Broad Street, where the ministers were then the Reverends W.H. Cornforth, Nicholas Boynes and T.G. Hartley. By the 1870s the chapel was full to capacity and land was purchased on the corner of what is now Mansfield Road and Woodborough Road for a new chapel, almost next door to the Shaw home. The foundation stone was laid on 22nd May 1871 and the new chapel was in use by August 1872, though members continued to support events at Broad Street and later at Tennyson Street where another new chapel was opened in 1874. John Shaw seems seldom to have attended after the death of his wife, but Mary Ellen, Lucy and Maud were all involved in teaching the various Sunday School classes on week nights as well as Sundays. Mary Ellen's typical weekly timetable, apart from her paid employment, included:

Wednesday: takes a Children's Meeting of up to 120 pupils, followed by a Chapel service.

Thursday: sometimes attends a Dorcas Meeting (sewing garments for the poor), followed by a Bible Class and a Prayer Meeting in the Chapel.

Friday: attends Bible Class and Prayer Meeting.

---

[8] Now Dagfa House School

Saturday: housework in the morning, then district visiting, delivering tracts etc.

Sunday: teaches in the Sunday School, then attends morning Chapel. Home to prepare dinner. In afternoon teaches an Infant Class, then a "ragged class" (pupils from the Ragged School). In evening, Chapel and sometimes another prayer meeting which she leads if nobody else is available.

It is a very busy schedule for a sixteen-year-old girl, but on top of all this she also gave music lessons twice a week, had French and music lessons herself and copied out the registry returns. Without a mother to restrain her, it is hardly surprising that by 1876 she was almost worn out. As the diaries progress, she often finishes an entry with the words "Depressed, discouraged, weary," or something similar; but she just as often writes simply, "Much helped." She prayed fervently to be able to cope with all her daily tasks, many of them self-imposed. On 9th June 1877 she records, "Went to 37 homes at night," and this was not uncommon. She visited the homes of her Sunday School pupils as well as other sick and needy people in the district, taking comforts and gifts of food. From an early age she must have witnessed all manner of degradation, human affliction and poverty, all of which she dealt with practically and calmly. For example,

> **June 3rd 1877:** Went to Dispensary with woman and child with bad arm. Saw it stitched in six places.
>
> **July 7th 1877:** Found a drunken man had been beating his wife. Fetched a policeman to him. Found another drunken man leaning his head on the bar of the fireplace.

The Sunday Schools were an exhausting but satisfying area of ministry; a hundred or more children from the deprived and poorer areas attended but they were often unresponsive and unruly and sometimes the young teacher lost control of them altogether and the class would have to be abandoned. But occasionally there was evidence of the Christian message getting through and she could feel the effort was all worthwhile. On October 11th 1875, Mary Ellen recorded in her diary the conversion of a child called Ada Hill:

> Last Wednesday at my meeting I was speaking of the necessity of giving our hearts to Jesus while we are young & I specially urged them to give their hearts to Christ as soon as possible telling them how willing he was for them

> to do so & how pleased he would be to make them his children. I noticed that several seemed to be particularly listening and amongst them was a little child about four or five. Today I met her in the street & asked her if she had thought of what I was telling her, she said she had done so & had given her heart to Jesus. Surprised and pleased I asked her how it was and she said that when she got home she went in the yard & knelt down & said, "Oh God I am very bad but I want to be good will you let me give you my heart for Jesus sake Amen" and so now she said she had given her heart to Jesus. I said and now you are his little child so she said yes, and in her childish simple faith she rested entirely in him and I cannot possibly know how much. My heart felt encouraged & helped for truly God had been very gracious, to him be all the glory.

In spite of the difficulties of controlling large classes, Mary Ellen emerged as a natural leader, able to address an audience clearly and concisely and hold people's attention. When, during a Christmas party, the young guests began to get restless at the boring commentary to some magic lantern slides, the adults appealed to her:

> The children began to get noisy and Miss Ward and Mrs Grundy with several others said they wished I would speak to them & explain the pictures myself. At first I felt very reluctant but at last I stood upon the form and explained each picture as best I could and on the whole they were much quieter. Mr Grundy proposed that a vote of thanks should be given to me and he spoke very kindly about our meetings during the year.

As time went on, her voluntary work increased: she would visit the County Jail and also the Workhouse, sometimes leading services for the children there. Sunday School "treats" had to be organised — and the funds raised to put them on. She notes sums of money solicited from chapel members and friends and her constant anxiety that there wouldn't be enough. This kind of fund-raising for good causes was to be a life-long preoccupation.

The Maypole Yard Project

In February 1877, Sunday classes for "ragged" boys were started at a room in Maypole Yard, off Clumber Street. Mary Ellen was chosen to be the principle teacher of these classes which met both afternoon and evening, and which proved to be much more difficult than anything she had tackled to date. Records kept by her indicate something of the standard of behaviour she was expected to deal with:

> **March 5th:** ...order bad, one hymn-book burnt and 3 books thrown at Mrs Fisher's head. Complaints from people living in the yard about disturbance after the boys were dismissed.
>
> **March 18th:** Boys in much disorder, gasses put out.
>
> **June 10th:** Henry P. in the middle of a hymn being sung very nicely threw a large bird egg across the room which hit another boy's head as intended and burst much to his discomfiture, while the others burst out laughing... Feeling this was too serious a thing to be passed over lightly we told him he would have to go from the Meeting. He rather unwillingly rose and sulkily walked to the door, then just turned and bursting into a rude laugh threw another. It fortunately passed Mrs Fisher and I but had the same effect as the previous one of sharply hitting another boy and disturbing the Meeting, but after his dismissal the order was very good.

This lad was obviously heading for real trouble and on 12th August she writes, "Went to the County Jail to see Harry P. with three others taken up for stealing." Sometimes the behaviour was so bad and the complaints so vociferous that a policeman had to be summoned to keep order in the Yard, and in April, Mary Ellen's father spoke to her about giving up the school, which depressed her greatly. In spite of all the problems, she wanted the work to succeed and pleaded with the Chapel Sunday School Committee to take responsibility for it, which eventually they agreed to do, only to decide that it was more trouble than it was worth.

The 1878 diary ends after a two-month gap. Mary Ellen explains that she is recovering from a bout of Scarlet Fever — probably caught during her district visiting — and that Lucy has been standing in for her at Bramcote. She had just begun to take up her Sunday School classes again, but reports receiving an official letter stating that the Ragged Class could no longer be held at Maypole Yard, and so the project came to an end.

Mary Ellen was not without her admirers — she was a pleasant-looking, intelligent, capable young woman. A lot of young men seem to have visited the Shaw home — perhaps a few more than might have been admitted had Mrs Shaw still been alive! She records her consternation when Edward Cross invited her to the Choir Party and her fear that an acceptance might compromise her. She sought advice from her beloved Bible Class leader,

Miss Ward, who sensibly suggested she should go to the party but insist upon paying for her own ticket. In spite of Mary Ellen's unusual independence for her age, she was still a motherless seventeen-year-old in the 1870s and obliged to protect her reputation. The friendship with Edward faded naturally away. By March 1877 two significant names begin to appear in her diary: Herbert Clarke, who would marry Lucy, and Samborne Cook. Sam later married Maud, but in 1877 it was Mary Ellen he courted, though she seems to have agonised over his (in her eyes) lack of religious commitment and this may have been the reason why the relationship faltered. However, she writes cryptically in her diary on August 13th and 15th, *"Mas dessik em"* (read backwards: Sam kissed me!)

Her illness seems to have finally alerted Mary Ellen's busy father to the extent of her exhaustion and over-work, because around August 1880 she went to France and he wrote her a loving letter whilst there, which she kept safe in her diary. In it he describes Herbert and Lucy and Sam and Maud all helping him with the registry returns late into the night (and no doubt accelerating their separate romances!) as,

> Infant mortality is very high just now. 17 last week and 9 this under 11 months. 108 births in July, and this month won't be far short at the present rate.

John Shaw mentions his own poor health, back pain and, ominously, "my old enemy", a persistent cough. Within two years, he was dead.

Chapter 2: The 1880s

On 9th November 1880 Lucy Shaw married Herbert Clarke at St Matthew's Church. Born in 1859, Herbert was the son of Helen (née Hunt) and John Clarke, hairdresser and tobacconist, who by 1880 was landlord of the Charlton Arms in Chilwell. Herbert began his working life in the lace trade, at the warehouse of Sir James Oldknow in Stoney Street, but at the time of the marriage, he was a brewer's traveller. He and Lucy set up home in Hutchinson Street. Back at the family home, on the 1881 census Mary Ellen, aged twenty-one, is recorded as a teacher of music and Maud, twenty, as housekeeper. Eighteen-year-old George had left home by now and appears to have been working in Ireland. Grandma Shaw continued to move between Nottingham and Newark.

John Shaw died on 24th January 1882 of *Phthisis Pulmonalis*, i.e. Consumption. He was only fifty-two. Two months later, Maud married Samborne Cook on her birthday, 28th March, at Mansfield Road Wesleyan Chapel. It was not long before Lucy and Herbert returned to live at 86 Mansfield Road when Herbert took over his late father-in-law's job as Registrar for St. Ann's District in 1883. Lucy gave birth to a son, Herbert Renshaw Clarke, in June 1882, followed by John, 1883, and Spencer in 1885. The children's baptisms were all at St Matthew's Church where Herbert was a member of the choir for fifty years. In the meantime, Maud and Sam had produced three daughters, Florence, Gertrude and Gladys. Grandma Shaw died in Newark on 21st March 1884. At some point during this period of change and upheaval, Mary Ellen left her family home and moved in with the Cooks.

When her next surviving diary begins on 31st December 1887, Mary Ellen, now aged twenty-eight, is living with Maud and Sam and their three girls at Scarborough Terrace, 49 Bentinck Road, Radford, moving with them later that year to 61 Bentinck Road. Samborne Cook was a successful chemist with a series of shops in the Radford area. He describes himself as a "Homeopathic and dispensing chemist" but in 1895 he also advertised dentistry. Born in Temple Cloud, Somerset, in 1857, Sam Cook was a clever young man who qualified as a chemist and druggist in 1881 and the same year opened his first shop at 76 Radford Road. We know he was in and around Nottingham as early as 1877, when it was Mary Ellen who attracted him to the Shaw household, though what first drew him to the area is a mystery. However, his subsequent marriage to Maud and an opening for his conspicuous entrepreneurial talents caused him to settle and soon people were snapping up pots of his patent "Carbolic Jelly" cure-all.[9]

The Olivers

This arrangement of Mary Ellen sharing the Cook household was not always a comfortable one, reflected in the fact that at this period she spent much of her time away, often staying overnight with the Renshaw aunts in Wilford or with the Olivers, a family of lace manufacturers at Fern Lodge, 4 Third Avenue, Sherwood Rise. Her special friend was (Hannah) Mary Oliver, with whom she was involved on various charitable committees, but Mary's married sister Lillie Marshall[10] was also a great friend and they all remained close for the rest of their lives. There was also a brother, "Mr Tom", and his wife Florence, whose children Mary Ellen later taught, and another branch of the family living in Villa Road. The Olivers seemed to understand Mary Ellen's difficulties as the spinster sister in her own family and the financial struggles which went with that, and provided her with bed and board whenever she wanted them. After Mrs Oliver was widowed, Mary Ellen would sometimes stay over to keep her company, as well as performing other helpful duties if her daughters were not available. Fern Lodge, at this period, became a substitute home for Mary Ellen, who otherwise occupied a room in her brother-in-law's household less than half a mile away.

Attached to the Oliver family were two Withers brothers, both doctors. Dr Oliver Withers practised on Beech Avenue, Sherwood Rise, and lived with two middle-aged aunts, Ann Oliver and Ellen Robinson. These two ladies were almost certainly the sisters of Mary's father, Thomas Oliver Snr.

---

[9] Peter Hammond has written a comprehensive account of Cook's career in "One of the most efficacious, agreeable, useful and popular remedies of the day" in *The Nottinghamshire Historian* No. 68, Spring/Summer 2002.

[10] Lillie was married to the architect Arthur Marshall and they had two daughters, Elaine and Doris.

which indicates that the Withers and Oliver families were already related. Oliver Withers' brother, Dr John Sheldon Withers, lived at Sale in Cheshire and was engaged to be married to Mary. Mary Ellen was very friendly with Oliver Withers and often mentions calling in to see him to discuss her own on-going studies and other matters. However, she developed a strong animosity towards his brother, probably because he threatened to take away her beloved Mary. She often expresses her dislike for "J.W." in her diary and notes that their mutual friends attempted to make her see reason.

Thorntons and Smiths

By this time she was teaching the children of at least six different families as well as giving lessons to her Cook nieces at home. These were mainly music lessons but also basic studies for very young children. For a number of years she taught members of the Thornton family at 58 Ropewalk — at this period two of the youngest children, Godfrey and Gertrude. She also escorted two older girls, Nina, sixteen, and Susie, thirteen, to other classes, public lectures and social events. Henry Edward Thornton was a banker with Smith & Co. An Evangelical by persuasion, his charitable interests were wide and "his home was a veritable centre for Church life in Nottingham."[11] On Sunday afternoons he took informal services in the wards of the General Hospital, near his home. He had eight children with his first wife, Catherine, whose death in 1906 was said at the time to be "equal to the loss of any three clergymen in the town." Mary Ellen was welcomed into this large, lively, Christian household and treated as a friend, without any sort of condescension. Through them she met and became involved with the Misses Smith at Wilford and in particular "Miss Alice" to whom she became especially attached.

The Smith banking family lived at Wilford House situated at the same end of Wilford village as the Renshaw aunts. The current generation consisted of Henry Abel Smith and his wife Elizabeth, sons Samuel Henry, Francis Abel and Robert Leslie Melville, and daughters Elizabeth Mary (known as Miss Smith, being the eldest), Marion, Alice Maude and Constance Helen. By the time of Mary Ellen's friendship with them, Samuel and his mother Elizabeth had died and Henry Abel Smith lived in the house with his daughters. Like

11 Obituary in *Southwell Diocesan Magazine*, December 1926

the Thorntons, the Smiths were much preoccupied with charitable projects and the girls shouldered the kind of parish duties incumbent upon the daughters of the local squire. As a child visiting her Wilford relations, Mary Ellen must have been aware of the family at the "big house". As an adult, she came more and more into contact with the Smith girls as they met in the context of the Girls' Evening Homes (see below) and other initiatives in Nottingham.

Mary Ellen and Miss Alice, as she always called her, became friends around 1888 and, perhaps sensing the immanent loss of Mary Oliver, Mary Ellen invested a lot emotionally in this friendship with Alice Smith — and also much physical energy. She spent more and more time at Wilford, attended the parish church and became involved in Bible Classes and Sunday School activities — all on top of her regular commitments at the Wesleyan Chapel. It was quite common for her to be called upon to take a class at Wilford at short notice because Miss Marion was busy or Miss Alice out of town. It has to be said that Mary Ellen was somewhat open to exploitation at this period — but she did all willingly out of devotion to "A.M.S." For all that, Alice appears to have been genuinely fond of Mary Ellen, sending her little gifts and corresponding with her almost daily.

At the Wesleyan Chapel, there was still plenty to occupy Mary Ellen: she took an Infant Class and Girl's Bible Class on Sundays, plus the Children's Bible Class on Thursday evenings, but she regularly attended other, Anglican, churches; as well as attendance at Wilford, she often went to an evening service at Emmanuel Church on Woodborough Road with Mary Oliver and the Withers brothers, though whether this is evidence of dissatisfaction with the Wesleyan tradition, or simply the desire to be with her friends, is a matter for conjecture. She certainly seems to have been restless, seeking for more than the Wesleyans could offer at this time and often refers in her diary to preachers she heard there as uninspiring, irritating or simply "poor". Her district visiting continued and there is evidence of her own calling to ministry strengthening at this period. On May 6th 1888 she gave what appears to have been her first formal address at a Chapel service, which affected her very much:

Sunday May 6: Fern Lodge to breakfast. Did some of my address on "Peter" in bed before getting up. Finished it after breakfast. Went to Mansfield Rd.

> Chapel. Heard Mr Ward preach. Went to Lucy's to dinner. Spencer wore his little blue frock — my making. Went to Infant Class but found Miss Harrison there so returned to Lucy's for quiet time before speaking in the Chapel. Went there at 3 o'clock. Spoke on "Peter", "Friendship & Temptation". Was much helped. Mary said I was very nervous.... Had a great struggle about going to [Emmanuel] Church at night. Went to Chapel instead & was much bored by the length of the sermon.

Three days later she notes with satisfaction: "Heard from two servants that they had been helped by my address on Sunday and was so thankful."

Girls' Evening Homes

Throughout this period, her most important voluntary work was with the Girls' Evening Homes movement. When George Ridding became the first Bishop of Southwell in 1884, he and his wife Laura vigorously supported all kinds of initiatives to save young women from drunkenness and prostitution. The provision of "evening homes" or clubs was one of these and by 1888 there were nine homes named for the Anglican churches where they were based, under the title of the Nottingham Church of England Temperance Society Girls' Evening Homes. However, a report in the *Southwell Diocesan Magazine* for 1891 refers to "the six original Girls' Evening Homes started in Nottingham in 1885 by Miss Paton, Miss Lewis and Miss Oliver with an undenominational committee" — a full year before the Anglican initiative. These were known simply as Nottingham Girls' Evening Homes with no reference to the Church of England or Temperance, but in the following years there seems to have been a great deal of overlap and co-operation among the different groups. Mary Ellen was a member of this non-denominational committee along with Octavia Liberty, Mary Ashwell, Minnie Ashwell, Miss Fletcher, Miss Kirkman and Miss Grundy. She was personally involved with the homes in St Ann's-street, Sherwood Street and Wool-alley for at least a decade, finding it a challenging but worthwhile work.

Lady Laura Ridding paid tribute to the success of the homes:

> The way in which the girls of the Nottingham factories and warehouses thronged into these Homes, itself proved the need of the homes and the necessity of providing one in every parish of the town. The object ... was to

> teach girls the truth about life, and provide with a good home those who had not a good home to go to. The Homes were made as bright and attractive as possible. Thrift was encouraged, and in connection with the Homes they had sewing, cooking, singing and other classes. Games were also allowed ... the temperance work ... had been especially successful, many of the girls becoming total abstainers.[12]

Drill or exercise classes were a regular feature of the homes and Mary Ellen herself conducted a number of these. They consisted of marching and synchronised manipulation of poles, clubs and dumb-bells and were a popular activity at this time, encouraging discipline, co-operation and providing healthy exercise for young women who might be cooped up in factories all day. Mary Ellen was pleased that at the annual prize-giving at the Albert Hall on 14th February 1888, Wool-alley Home took first prize for musical drill and St Ann's for singing. Music was an important element and Mary Ellen played the piano for them, sometimes calling on the additional services of her musical family:

> **Thursday April 12:** Called at Lucy's and persuaded her and Herbert to go to St Ann's Home. They came and the girls were delighted. They sang two duets and old Mr Clarke played the violin while we did the drilling. I went home encouraged and thankful.

But the girls could be quite unruly and at the end of a long day teaching, this could prove exhausting and discouraging. Also they couldn't be relied upon always to behave when taken out on "treats":

> **Friday June 30th:** ...went to meet our girls and we went to Burton Joyce — had tea and all went off well until near the end of evening. I found some girls in the public house — had a bother and great quarrelling, excitement and noise in getting home... Very tired and thankful to arrive safely without accident.

Obviously the temptation proved too great on this occasion! It was an on-going concern to the committee, as Octavia admitted:

> The time in which our work is perhaps the most difficult is Goose Fair, when, in spite of rabbit suppers, toffee making, and other entertainments, our efforts to keep the girls away from the dangerous attractions of the town on Saturday night do not meet with the success we desire.[13]

---

12 *Southwell Diocesan Magazine,* 1888.

13 Report of the 6 Girl's Evening Homes *Southwell Diocesan Magazine* 1893.

In spite of all difficulties, Mary Ellen went to endless trouble for "her" girls, speaking to the mother of one about the perils of her daughter going on the stage, and rescuing another girl called Phoebe from a public house in Lees Yard where she had been injured. Mary Ellen was never judgmental in these circumstances, recognising that many of these girls knew no better, and she just tried to help. Often she entertained them to tea-parties in her own room at Bentinck Road and showed an interest in their concerns.

There was also an institution known as "The Refuge"[14], which was a special interest of Alice Smith's, and Mary Ellen occasionally took classes there. After Alice went abroad, Mary Ellen 'inherited' this responsibility.

What with the Homes, church commitments, and her fragmented, insecure working life (children grew up and were sent to school), and constantly on the move between home, Fern Lodge and Wilford, Mary Ellen was often tired out, anxious and depressed. Several times she records her friends begging her to do less:

> **Tuesday May 29:** After Edith's lesson I went to see Dr Stewart professionally. He begs me to give up all Sunday-work and rest more. How can I?

It was difficult for some of her wealthier friends to understand that she had to earn her own living. On one occasion, when invited to Ingoldmells with Mary and Lillie, she sadly, "declined because I am to teach." However, frenetic activity seems to have been a personality trait, and throughout her life, Mary Ellen was always juggling many causes, duties and enthusiasms, which was bound to take its toll.

1888 was an emotionally turbulent year: the diary has uncharacteristic gaps and pages torn out of it. The crisis point came when Mary Oliver married John Sheldon Withers. On July 8th Mary Ellen confides to its pages, "had a good cry about Mary leaving". On Mary's last Sunday in Nottingham there were many tears shed on both sides and she couldn't bring herself even to speak to the man who was taking her friend away from her. Her description of Mary's wedding at St Andrew's Church on Mansfield Road does not even mention the bridegroom! The girls from the Evening Homes attended the service and they had a celebratory picnic in Bakewell afterwards which cheered Mary Ellen up somewhat: "Had great fun going home and we sang nearly all the way. Auld Lang Syne etc." But it was the

[14] The House of Refuge for Women, Chaucer St.

end of an era, not least because Mary Ellen no longer had an excuse to take refuge at Fern Lodge.

During this upsetting period she relied more and more upon the support of Alice Smith and her sisters, so it was a double blow when at the beginning of October the Smiths left Wilford House to go abroad. Miss Marion was to die tragically a year later of typhoid, in Naples, and her father only three months later of the same disease.

Goolds and Coys

There were other friends to help fill the gaps left by Mary and Alice. The Goold family lived at Stratford House on Shakespeare Street. Joseph[15] and Clara Goold were popular music teachers, as were at least two of their nine children. Mary Ellen took lessons with Mrs Goold and arranged for several of her pupils (including Lucy's two eldest boys) to have lessons with her too, and they became good friends. Kate Goold had married into the Coy family and was a young widow with a little boy, Chris. Her in-laws, Mary, Annie, Margaret and John Coy became friends of Mary Ellen and there are strong hints of an "understanding" at one time between Mary Ellen and John which ended acrimoniously. During that difficult autumn of 1888, Mary Ellen stayed with the Coys at Sproxton, where she was able to rest and collect her thoughts together. In later years she visited them regularly at Leicester.

Throughout the year, in spare moments, Mary Ellen had been painstakingly making garments — not for the poor, but for Lucy's children, in particular for three-year-old Spencer. Mary Ellen struggled with such tasks but was helped by Lillie Marshall who cut out the patterns and gave her sewing lessons. In December, for the first time, she writes of her nagging unease about Lucy:

> **Friday December 7:** Troubled about Lucy's home and the boys not being kept more tidy.

Lucy had her own problems and things were to get very much worse.

---

[15] Inventor of the Twin Elliptic Pendulum Harmonograph to measure harmonic vibrations.

Chapter 3: The 1890s

Eight years pass before the next surviving diary. Aunt Eliza Pocklington died in September 1888 amid difficulties in the family which she tearfully confided to Mary Ellen a few days before her death. She was the last link with the older Shaws, but it is to be expected that the younger generation continued to keep in touch with their Newark cousins. Lucy and Herbert had a daughter, Kathleen Alice Luberta (known as "Kalcie"), on 27th October 1889; but less than a year later on 5th October 1890, five-year-old Spencer died of diabetes and a "cerebral effusion". Lucy's already fragile disposition was shaken: she suffered from depression and turned more and more to alcohol for relief. The birth of Nora Carmen on 9th August 1895 only exacerbated her psychological turmoil as the new baby was sickly and unresponsive. All this was apparent to her sisters, but all gestures of concern were repulsed; Herbert seemed to be in denial about Lucy's state of mind, and it was very difficult for them to help. Mary Ellen kept an eye on the children, drawing the boys, Bertie and Jack, into musical activities at Chapel when she could, and sewing garments for the two little girls.

The end of the farm

Meanwhile, at Wilford, the Smith family had left Wilford House for good, and the aunts were getting older. Aunt Sarah Ann was unexpectedly widowed on 4th March 1888 when her husband, John Clements, died suddenly in Wilford Church, during the morning service. An inquest was held but the verdict was "Death from natural causes." There were no children of the marriage. Rachel and Rebecca Renshaw continued to run the farm together with Mary Ellen helping with the accounts.[16] Their step-father, William Spencer, had left them some 60 acres of barley, oats, turnips, mangolds and grass, an orchard, seven milking cows and some sheep, three cart horses, a mare and a pony. There were also 18 acres of arable land worth £138 in rent and two cottages. In 1894 a small piece of

16 The account book is in the Nottinghamshire Archives, ref. DD2553/3/1

the land — 2 roods and 16 perches, to be precise — was sold off to the M.S.L. Railway Co. for £35. The aunts were a redoubtable pair but their health was failing. Rebecca died first on 23rd June 1892, aged sixty-six. Rachel carried on for another three and a half years, dying on 6th November 1895, aged sixty-seven, and the farm, which had been in the Harpham and Renshaw family for at least a hundred years was put up for sale.

Mary Ellen's diary for 1896 begins in a flurry of activity as the family convened to prepare the farm for auction and dispose of the contents. It was an emotionally charged time and there was friction between Mary Ellen, Lucy and Maud, and the two husbands. The auction, which was conducted by Mr F. W. Kidd of Thurland Street, took place on 22nd and 23rd January — a bleak time of year for a bleak undertaking.

> **Thursday January 23:** Went to Wilford with Madge & Sam at 9.30 for the Sale of Furniture. Bitterly cold day. Great many people at the sale. I sat on a cushion on the yard wall with Edith [Petchell, one of the servants] behind Mr Kidd. Bought box and hearthrug. Had some hot tea with Annie Cross. In afternoon saw cattle sold. When Maggie was sold I broke down and cried bitterly. Had an awful headache. We all went to Aunt's to tea. I rode home with Sam and Maud... Home at 7.30 very done up... Feel very low about Wilford. To go no more to the dear little house.

She was very distressed at the loss of her beloved aunts and the farm which had been her haven for years. She continued to visit Aunt Sarah Ann at least once a week, but as she wrote in her diary:

> **Saturday May 9:** Went to Wilford and had tea with Aunt ... felt so sorry to see the dear old house and not be able to go into it — thought of Aunt Rebecca.

She became obsessed with the fate of the mare, Maggie, whom she was convinced had been sold to a cruel master, and begged both her brothers-in-law to buy her back, a futile campaign which continued to irritate them both and cause bad feeling for some months. It was as if she was desperately trying to hold on to something belonging to a happier past.

Mary Ellen still lived with Maud and Sam and their three girls at 61 Bentinck Road. She still taught at the Ropewalk, but now her main charge was thirteen-year-old Gertie Thornton. Susi and Nina were now grown up and Susi married. Tom and Florence Oliver's children, Tommy and Gordon, at Southfield House, Bramcote were now her pupils, as were Annie Grimshaw, daughter of the Wesleyan Minister, Hilda Fish and nieces Florence and Gertie Cook who were thirteen and eleven respectively. Mary Ellen was now thirty-six and still had to earn her living, though the death of Aunt Rachel eased things somewhat financially. Rachel left her nephew and nieces £50 apiece plus a share in the residue of her estate — though not to be paid until twelve months after her death. Informal bequests had also been made — jewellery, silver and household linen etc., some of which they sold; Mary Ellen notes in her diary how much she and Maud received for china, books, furniture etc. There was even a quantity of port wine to be disposed of. Mary Ellen refused to keep it and sold it to a friend for £1.4s whereupon Lucy and Herbert accused her of meanness, which hurt her. Presumably they thought she should have given it to them. An argument ensued with Herbert over the final settling of the estate, whereby Mary Ellen stood to lose out on some of her share. In the end she had to appeal to Mr Eking, the lawyer, who took her side and made sure she received her full legacy of some £180. Her sisters' affairs were in the hands of their husbands, but as a single woman, Mary Ellen had to stand up for herself!

Her "girls"

At Chapel she still took the Infant Class, Girl's Bible Class and sundry children's services. She also had a growing ministry of preaching in other Sunday Schools and chapels both in Nottingham and further afield. In this she was supported by the Rev J. Grimshaw who gave her weekly lessons in theology, amongst other subjects, probably in exchange for the music lessons she gave his daughter Annie. The Girls' Evening Homes flourished and she was still involved at Sherwood Street, as well as new branches at Norton Street, Windsor Street (where the girls were "a rough wild young set") and St Mark's ("Bad time, the girls so fearfully unruly"). She continued to teach them drill and singing several nights a week.

Hucknall Girl's Society

In addition, she was also teaching a class in Hucknall. Hucknall Girl's Society was begun around 1890 through the efforts of Mrs Needham Ball of

Beacon Hill. It was run on similar lines to the Evening Homes, under the umbrella of the parish church, and most of its members would have been girls working locally in the textile trades. By 1898 the Society had 160 members. Henry Thornton's name is connected with it, as well as the Smiths of Bramcote Hall, the Marsden family and Mr J. E. Ellis, MP for Rushcliffe, a local colliery manager and benefactor. Hucknall Institute and Coffee Tavern was a popular meeting place for societies such as this, being a more neutral venue than the church hall, and the *Hucknall Star & Advertiser* faithfully reported the Girl's Society's annual sale of work when "the stalls were heavily laden with articles of a useful character" each December. The annual entertainment and prize-giving in May required larger premises and grew so popular that by 1895 the Public Hall was required for the display of musical and drilling skills. Detailed reviews of these events over the years allow one to gauge the extent of Mary Ellen's involvement. She shared the work with a Miss Brocklehurst, who is referred to as "the lady missioner". From 1893 (probably the first full-scale event) appreciative remarks on the drilling items under the instruction of Miss M. E. Shaw are made. Mary Ellen herself had to work hard to keep the girls' interest with the latest techniques and in March of 1896 she records that "Mary Cannity came to teach me some Club Drill. Very much exhausted..." Her dedication paid off, though. In May, the local reporter, in an extensive article noted:

> The chief feature of the programme ... was the drilling exercises, which numbered three. The first was by 11 girls who went through the exercise with "Poles" in a finished style; the second, "Dumb Bells", was more arduous, but was completed with precision by 13 girls; while the third, "Indian Clubs", was well executed, the performance of which is especially worthy of mention, as it was a most difficult and intricate piece; the whole proving how assiduous Miss Shaw had been for the girls to reach the pitch of excellence they had attained.[17]

In December that year, Mary Ellen was learning the latest "Ball Drill" to teach her students and notes in her diary that the balls cost 3/6 per dozen. By 1898 the Society had 160 members but the local press seems to have lost interest after this so it is not possible to work out when Mary Ellen's involvement ceased.

---

17 *Hucknall Star & Advertiser*, 11 May 1896.

Teaching the Hucknall girls added considerably to her weekly responsibilities, although she was paid to take this class by Mrs Ball. In Nottingham she was as busy as ever, flying from one Home to another, putting on events for the girls and raising funds for them. Sometimes she could persuade friends to "sponsor" a particular case, and she notes that her old friend Dr Oliver Withers gave her ten shillings for a girl called Clara Radford, which she issued at the rate of 2/6 per month. Even this small sum would have been sufficient to make a difference and perhaps keep a vulnerable girl from destitution, which was all too common. On one occasion she recounts a little supper given for some of the girls:

> **Wednesday June 17:** At 8 o'clock eight girls came to supper with me, and afterwards we had music and singing. Sarah Hall could not come because her mother had pawned her clothes.

She was always doing her best to improve their circumstances: Mary Dale, whom she had placed in an orphanage in 1888 for her own good, was about to go into service and Mary Ellen bought her a new dress. When the job didn't work out, it was she who took Mary back to the agency, made sure she was alright and had a new position to go to. Sometimes she was able to get recommendations to send sickly young women to the Convalescent Home[18] at Castle Donington for a rest. The patients often lacked even the basics, such as night-dresses or decent underwear. If there wasn't enough in the kitty, then she plundered her own wardrobe:

> **Wednesday October 7:** Ada Dexter called and I arranged for her to go to Castle Donington and lent her pocket handkerchiefs, night-dress, black bag, shawl, slippers etc.

Mary Ellen enjoyed nice clothes; she was very particular about them, and of course it was necessary for her to keep up appearances in the homes of her wealthier pupils, but in the end her girls came first. She also organised seaside holidays for them at Old Orchard House, farmhouse home of the Vickers family, at Ingoldmells, a few at a time, taking along as many friends and family as she could muster to help. It must be remembered that Ingoldmells was a very small village in those days, offering the greatest possible contrast to the city for the grateful visitors; but these excursions

---

[18] Nottingham Convalescent Home for Females, in connection with the Nottingham Town and County Social Guild.

never seemed to give Mary Ellen herself much rest. Wherever she went she found herself leading 'cottage meetings', visiting the poor and preaching at local services. This entry for Sunday August 23rd is typical:

> We had breakfast at 8.30 and then I went to Ingoldmells village by the road with Mrs Goold and Annie Grundy. I told the Sunday School children "The Angel of Love". In the afternoon I went to the Chapel and conducted the service. Spoke on Nehemiah. Then we had a Class meeting and all spoke. After tea, we all went to Chapel. Mrs Goold played the harmonium. Mary [Coy] sang a solo and Mary and Annie sang a duet from Sankey and I gave the sermon (4 Mark) on the Thorny Ground. We had 50 people present and a good service. Then Mary and I went to see Mrs Davidson and home over the fields. Supper and then we all sang in the kitchen to Mrs Vickers and Mr Vickers.

Nephew Jack Clarke, aged thirteen, also came and sang. A pupil of Mrs Goold's, he was already showing great talent as a performer and was to become a very successful opera singer in later life.

Octavia Liberty was Honorary Secretary of the Evening Homes at this period, and Mary Ellen was friendly with the whole family at Tintagel, Mapperley Road. She was also a frequent guest at 306 Mansfield Road, the home of the Marsdens, who were staunch members of the Wesleyan Chapel and deeply involved in voluntary activities in the area. It was natural that many of her circle of friends were people with a similar concern for the poor and disadvantaged in the city. Dr Philip Boobbyer was appointed Medical Officer of Health in 1889 and spent almost forty years seeking to improve public health conditions, in particular the building of proper sewerage in the lower St Ann's and Sneinton areas, which were frequently ravaged by typhoid and infantile diarrhoea.[19] In 1896 Boobbyer and his wife Annie were living on 24 Forest Road where Mary Ellen often visited them. Something which I think worth noting here, is that many of these social concerns and endeavours crossed denominational religious boundaries: all flavours of the Church of England, Wesleyans, Baptists and Plymouth Brethren were just a few of the churches and chapels represented, all working together for a common cause, which was the alleviation of poverty and suffering in Nottingham.

---

[19] For more about Philip Boobbyer, see "Nottingham's health pioneer" by Denise Amos in *The Nottinghamshire Historian* No. 69, Autumn/Winter 2002.

Sale, Erdington and "Fred"

The two Dr Withers and their families were now living in Sale and Mary Ellen was a frequent guest in both households. She had long since forgiven Sheldon Withers for carrying off "her" Mary! Oliver Withers had also married a Mary, and both families had small children. They all continued to encourage and support Mary Ellen in her work and other responsibilities — and it was to them she escaped for a few days amidst the sadness of selling the Wilford farm. They made no demands upon her but sought to entertain her and forced her to relax. The Goolds were also close friends and during this period she went to them for Sunday lunch most weeks, taking their little grandson, Chris Coy, to Sunday School with her in the afternoon. Visits to Kate Coy's in-laws in Leicester were also frequent and she records giving addresses at Sunday Schools in the Belgrave area during these visits.

In April 1896 a visit to the Bentons, some friends at Erdington, near Birmingham, seriously raised Mary Ellen's hopes of marriage, only to have them cruelly dashed a few months later. Whilst there, she renewed an old acquaintance with two bachelor brothers, Fred and Will Wright, who ran a nursery garden. Fred Wright declared his love for her and convinced her sufficiently of his intentions that she returned to Nottingham full of hopes for the future. "Such a new experience..." she writes, "may God guide me to act rightly." She was very excited to receive her "first love letter" from Fred on May 3rd, and could not resist telling all her friends about him. However, seeds of disappointment were already sewn. Will Wright appears to have interfered in the affair and Mary Ellen was already a little bothered by Fred's lack of Christian commitment. There was also the problem of conducting the romance long-distance — her friends the Bentons were unable to put her up again at this time and Fred claimed to be unable to get away to visit her in Nottingham. Maud did her best, twice inviting him to stay with them, but each time he refused. Was Fred beginning to have second thoughts, or at least being adversely influenced by his brother? He continued to write but entries in the diary such as, "Letter from Fred explaining Will's lies. Made me very angry..." and "very sad letter from Fred. Felt troubled about him", did not bode well and by June he was suggesting they should cease their correspondence. On June 10th she wrote that she was, "Very troubled and hurt by Fred's letter of Monday," and wrote to him for the last time. This was obviously a huge disappointment and Mary Ellen was very depressed by the way her hopes of love and marriage had simply fizzled out. As a result she threw herself even harder into work, but she continued to think sadly of Fred for a long time afterwards.

The open road

In spite of all the heartache, Mary Ellen found a new pleasure and freedom that year — she bought a bicycle! The cycling craze was on and many of her friends and family, including the Cooks and Clarkes, had already bought bicycles and were going out for a sociable 'spin' every spare moment. As early as February she was "wondering if it would be wise to have a bicycle." For some weeks she contemplated the shiny new machines on show in Pearson's window and confessed that she was "longing to have one". After sounding out the opinions of various people — including her Minister! — she began to have lessons at Pearson's. By the 6th lesson she reports that she can ride alone for the first time and soon she has graduated to having lessons on her very own bicycle, outside, on the roads. The new occupation also required appropriate clothing: "Madge has begun to wear knickers," she notes on March 21st — not underwear, but cycling attire of the Bloomer variety! And before long, Mary Ellen too is pinning up her hems and taking delivery of a pair of "Navy Blue Strong Linen Knickers." Freedom of movement was only one of the benefits of the bicycle boom. After a few false starts — "Had a bad fall on Goldsmith Street and made a black eye and hurt my thumb" — she was soon cycling everywhere and thoroughly enjoying the independence it gave her. She was also very keen to convert others to this new form of transport and was giving lessons to all and sundry. The bicycle signalled an important means of self-sufficiency for girls and women, especially women like Mary Ellen who were often required to be out alone after dark. She could put her bike on the train if she had appointments out of town, cycle to her meeting, then come back and cycle home from the station without the need of an escort.

Between her many appointments, Mary Ellen often snatched a bite to eat at the Mikado or the Eagle cafés on Long Row. She also frequented the

Nottingham Subscription Library at Bromley House where she could change her books, write letters, and sometimes even have a little doze.

The death of Lucy

Lucy had been giving cause for concern for years, but the crisis came in 1896. Photographs of Lucy, even in her late thirties, show a thin, slightly-stooping, exhausted-looking woman who could be much younger. In her youth, Lucy was evidently capable and outspoken. At the age of nineteen, she wrote a strong letter to the local newspaper[20] protesting against the charge that she and other ladies had made false statements about certain candidates in the local School Board Elections. She challenged the Chairman of the Notts. School Board in print, and an embarrassed Mary Ellen referred to it in her diary as "Lucy's disgraceful letter". She stepped into the breach and taught her sister's pupils when Mary Ellen caught Scarlet Fever in 1877 and was also a talented singer on the concert platform. My point is that Lucy's fragile appearance belied a strong character and intellect, which somehow became eroded over the years. It seems as though her natural spirit was crushed by childbirth, the death of her youngest son and finally the birth of Nora, who had learning difficulties. She couldn't cope with her growing family, which is why Mary Ellen took it upon herself to provide for the youngest children to the extent of making clothes for Spencer and later for Kalcie.

That Lucy was an alcoholic seems to have been a recognised fact for years, though they wouldn't have used that word, in fact Mary Ellen never directly admits to her sister's intemperance in her diary, only to the effects of it.

> **Sunday January 19:** Herbert and I had a serious talk on subject of "Drink" and I strongly urged him to act more decidedly with regard to Lucy and become a teetotaller himself.

In May she notes, "Baby and Lucy looking wretchedly poorly!" Lucy was probably deeply depressed. Herbert's solution was to take refuge in his office. By August, Mary Ellen admits she was "much troubled" because the children were being neglected.

---

20 "The Lady Canvassers at the Last Election" in *Nottingham & Midland Counties Daily Express*, Friday 4 May 1877.

> **Sunday August 9:** Lucy and I had a few words about Kalcie. I am much distressed about Lucy!

Their brother George and his family visited from abroad that summer and he and Mary Ellen discussed the problem at length. In company Lucy could be bright and sociable, but her home situation seems to have become unbearable to her and it was impossible for anyone to help. Things got worse, and she was several times brought home after falling down drunk in the street.

> **Friday October 30:** Heard that Lucy had had another fall and had been brought home in a cab from Sherwood Rise with her face badly cut. Very sorrowful about her.

Mary Ellen's diary stops abruptly on December 21st which indicates a family crisis, and we know that Lucy died on 28th. Her death certificate, which her own husband, as Registrar, was obliged to make out and sign, uncompromisingly gives cause of death as "Delirium Tremens and Exhaustion". Mary Ellen was present at the death. It does not take much imagination to fathom the awfulness of Lucy's demise and the shame and distress it involved for her family and friends. She was only thirty-eight. The four surviving children were Herbert ("Bertie"), fourteen, Jack thirteen, Kalcie seven and Nora fifteen months.

Maud and Sam had recently moved to Forest Grove House, a pleasant detached house off Mount Hooton Road which reflected Sam's business success, and Mary Ellen had moved with them. Living with Sam and Maud had always been a rather uneasy arrangement and tensions periodically erupted into rows, which had caused Mary Ellen to rely on her friends for home comforts and for somewhere to relax when she wasn't tearing around on her bicycle from one pupil to another or caring for the Evening Home girls. With Lucy's death, another possibility opened up, that of returning to her childhood home at 86 Mansfield Road to help care for her motherless nephews and nieces, though this was not a decision she made lightly. She and Herbert had had their disagreements over the years and such an arrangement could be open to misinterpretation by outsiders. We are not sure exactly when it happened, but not very long after Lucy's death, Mary Ellen left the Cooks and moved in with the Clarkes, a decision which marked a new phase in her life.

1. Grandma Spencer, late Renshaw, nee Harpham

2. Mary Ellen's mother, Elizabeth Shaw, nee Renshaw

3. Rebecca Renshaw

4. Rachel Renshaw

5. Wesleyan Chapel, Mansfield Road, c. 1900

6. Annie Maud Shaw

7. Alice Smith

8. Clarke Family c. 1890. Back L-R: John & Helen Clarke, Herbert & Lucy
Front L-R: Bertie, Kalcie & Jack.

9. Welbeck c.1916. L-R: Unknown, Lady Victoria Cavendish-Bentinck,
The Duchess of Portland, Mary Ellen Shaw, Unknown.

10. Welbeck c.1908. Mothers' and Babies' Guild outing.

Another Snapshot of Miss Shaw's Class at Welbeck Abbey.

11. Welbeck 1912. Men's Bible Class outing (*Methodist Recorder*).

Chapter 4: The later years

Mary Ellen was very much attached to the Clarke children; she had watched over them during Lucy's slow, painful demise, making sure the little girls were respectably clothed and providing the boys with their first books. But she did not move into the house at Mansfield Road as a substitute mother to them; she received her board and lodging from her brother-in-law and continued with her teaching and voluntary work, helping out with the registry returns as required, and for this she was paid. This was a valuable help to Herbert as his registry area now extended right up to Mapperley Hospital. If there was an epidemic, such as the terrible 'flu epidemic of 1918, there would be many deaths to record and they had to work all hours to get the returns done. She was sometimes called upon to act as a witness if Herbert had to conduct a marriage, too, presumably in the office at the end of the yard!

She may not have been a natural mother-figure, but she did help fill the gap Lucy's death had left, supporting the young Clarkes throughout their childhood years and beyond. Letters to Kalcie from her father, between 1897 and 1914 acknowledge how their "Auntie Mary" wrote regularly to all of them (she was a great letter writer) when they were away from home and was involved in decision-making for their future. In her 1916 diary Mary Ellen often refers to Herbert as "Father" or "Daddy", a habit adopted in the early years when the girls were tiny, which simply stuck. But the names Herbert and Mary Ellen used for one another do give the impression of an affectionate and united family.

Bertie and Jack both attended Nottingham High School. Bertie, the eldest, was something of a tearaway in his youth but he was later taken into his Uncle Sam Cook's chemist's business as a partner, and eventually took it over altogether, Sam and Maud having no sons of their own. Jack was a much gentler, attractive, artistic boy who rather suffered from his older brother's reputation at school. Both boys sang in the choir at St Matthew's Church with their father, but Jack, encouraged by Mary Ellen, developed exceptional musical ability and became a professional opera singer trained in Italy by Baron Negri. He sang at Covent Garden and Milan and later became a well-known actor on Broadway. Kalcie attended the Girls' High School but was not especially academic, being more of a practical person and capable of doing beautiful needlework. She had the benefit of a year's "finishing" at Neufchatel in Switzerland in 1907. She did not get on especially well with her Aunt Mary, claiming her to be a 'martinet' — much too fussy and particular about things. Mary Ellen paid her 6d apiece to iron her pin-tucked white silk blouses which she put on clean every day, and as they had to be done with flat irons heated on the kitchen range, one can imagine the difficulties of achieving the required standard. Nora was a slow learner and was sent away to school in Hunstanton when she was older. She found it difficult to undertake even simple tasks on her own so it was a red letter day when she did manage to accomplish something — her aunt wrote triumphantly in her diary in 1916, "Nora cooked supper!" She required constant supervision and would never be able to live independently, but during the war Mary Ellen was able to find a succession of simple jobs for her in various voluntary organisations.

The Portlands

Many of the charitable enterprises Mary Ellen was involved with depended not only upon the energies of concerned women like herself for success, but also upon the patronage and support of local dignitaries and the aristocracy. The Evening Homes enjoyed the Presidency of Lady Laura Ridding during Bishop Ridding's time in Southwell, leaving a significant gap when she left the Diocese after his death in 1904. Later, Mrs F. C. Smith of Bramcote Hall[21], Lady Arthur Black, or Lady Maud Rolleston of Watnall Hall were courted to do the honours at public anniversaries. Mary Ellen wanted only the best for her girls and on 25th November 1916 she went joyfully to the Girl's High School to welcome Lady Victoria Cavendish-Bentinck, daughter of the Duke and Duchess of Portland, as the new President of the Girl's Evening Homes.

---

21 Harriet, wife of Frederick Chatfield Smith, a cousin of the Wilford Smiths and one-time MP of North Nottinghamshire. Her name appears on the foundation stone of the Coffee Tavern at Hucknall.

The Portlands were well known in Nottinghamshire for their benevolence towards the poor and disadvantaged, and the popular Duchess Winifred, with her imposing height, glamorous appearance and winning manner became a warm supporter of Mary Ellen's campaigns, providing a useful media focus, as well as essential financial support. Indeed, the Duchess's involvement became a vital element in the success of Mary Ellen's latest and most impressive initiative — "Miss Shaw's Men's Bible Class".

Miss Shaw's Men's Bible Class

Mary Ellen had for many years been involved in work with women and girls but in 1900 she had what can only be described as a vision to help the poor working men of the city. The men invariably held the purse-strings in the family; if the contents of that purse went straight to the pub instead of into the home, their wives and children suffered. If those men could be given a sense of self-worth and a moral responsibility for their families, much of the rescue work for women would not be necessary. This was to be accomplished by weaning the men off strong drink and tobacco and offering good fellowship and Bible principles as a substitute. The beginnings of the Bible Class are legendary: Mary Ellen began by inviting 100 men to tea at the Wesleyan Schoolroom on Mansfield Road on the second Saturday in December 1900. Lady Laura Ridding gave a ten-minute address on the subject, "How do we fight our devils?" and invited them to a Bible class the following day. They all said they would come, but on Sunday only two turned up, brothers Oliver and William Booth.[22] But Mary Ellen was undaunted and went ahead anyway. Gradually the class grew — and grew. She had at first targeted the fathers of the infants in her Sunday School class but they soon began to be drawn from a wider area and in 1912 a Mansfield branch was also established at the request of the Duke and Duchess of Portland, who supported the enterprise from the beginning.

By 1907, when the *Nottingham Daily Express* reported on the men's annual dinner at the Mikado Café on 31st January, to which Her Grace the Duchess was invited, there were 90 members. By 1914, at the outbreak of war, there were nearly 500. The 1907 dinner was especially significant. Mary Ellen was joined on the platform by the Thorntons, Councillor W. E.

[22] William Booth was still a member 50 years later.

Carey, the Revd. Rosslyn Bruce of Clifton and others. Twelve-year-old Nora presented the Duchess with a bouquet[23] and Herbert and Jack Clarke, along with the Dolce Glee Singers, provided the musical entertainment. Those facts were all noted in the newspaper, but for Mary Ellen it was a much more emotional and triumphant occasion and she wrote a full account of it to circulate to her subscribers — for, as ever, she relied heavily upon financial support from well-wishers. In previous years, Lady Maud Rolleston had given the address, but the presence of the lovely Duchess was a real coup and one which was to establish the Men's Bible Class firmly in the public eye. Mary Ellen describes the arrival of the Duchess:

> She came direct from Welbeck in her beautiful motor car. Mr Thornton met her at the door of the Café and brought her upstairs to me. I was waiting for her on the big square landing. The Manageress of the Café had kindly ordered red felt to be put down in the shop, for the Duchess to tread upon. I wish I could describe to you how beautiful she looked. I took her to the private sitting room to take off her cloak and I can't tell you how sweet and delightful she was. She wore evening dress, of very fine black lace (exquisite). On her neck was a pearl necklace (the famous pearls you may have heard of) and on her hair she wore a wreath of leaves, on two of which were small diamonds. You will probably remember that she has a very graceful figure. She really looked most lovely, and what a wondrous smile she has! I don't wonder she wins people's hearts. She certainly won mine...

She goes on to describe how she had written to Her Grace "in fear and trembling" to ask her to come and address the men; but she accepted willingly and furthermore offered the men the choice of a visit to the gardens at Welbeck in the summer or a tea at the Mikado for their womenfolk. Mary Ellen comments:

> The Duchess wished the men to decide the matter themselves. We put it to the vote. Fifteen only voted for the Women's Tea, and nearly seventy for the visit to Welbeck (selfish creatures!). I can only plead as an excuse for them that they acted honestly, and as one man, a kind of leader among them said, "We might never get the chance agen of seeing the Dook's place."

The Duchess was more generous than they — she announced that evening that not only would the visit go ahead in July, but a tea for the women would

---

23 The men had contributed a penny each towards the bouquet .

be held too, at her own expense. This open-handed gesture was typical of her.

> Now has not the Duchess been absolutely splendid? I am quite overwhelmed by her kindness.... While I rejoice with the men at the prospect of their summer visit to Welbeck, I am even more pleased about the Women's Tea which we hope to have on 7th March at the Mikado Café — because it will be so nice to have a woman from every home, and I think will strengthen the Class. [24]

The visit to Welbeck was a significant one for the Class, and I have printed the whole of Mary Ellen's report below, because it tells much of the generosity of the Portlands, life at Welbeck at that period, the behaviour of the men in their unaccustomed surroundings and, most importantly, the setting of the corner-stone to the Bible Class — the Duchess herself as their President — which was to endure long after Mary Ellen Shaw's death.

An Account of the Men's Visit to Welbeck Abbey, Saturday, August 3rd 1907
by invitation of the Duke and Duchess of Portland

> We left Nottingham Station by the 12.10 train. There were 90 men and twelve ladies and gentlemen, Sunday School workers. The day before, the Nottm. Station Master received the following telegram from Captain Amory, the Duke's Secretary:— "The Duke of Portland will be much obliged if you will kindly do all you can for Miss Shaw's men tomorrow." We found there were ten or twelve carriages reserved for our special use, and as the station was much crowded (it being the Saturday before Bank Holiday) this was a great help. My brother-in-law, Mr H. Clarke, managed the distribution of the tickets. When we got to Creswell, there were seven or eight Brakes ready to take us to the Abbey. The day was hot & beautiful and the men's spirits very high. They quickly jumped into the Brakes, and as the drivers cracked their whips and we started, one man began to sing the Glory Song[25] and the others joined in eagerly. It amused me greatly. How we all enjoyed the drive past the pretty water, by Creswell Crags, and through the underground tunnel to the Abbey. I have never driven with such a merry party. We were taken to the

---

24 A Monday evening class for wives, mothers, sisters & sweethearts of the men was later established, run by Mrs Crumpton, Mrs Maule and Mrs Richards.

25 "Oh that will be glory for me" by US hymn writer Charles H. Gabriel.

back entrance so that the men might dismount near the Servants' Hall where a most excellent luncheon was provided for them. The Sunday School workers had their luncheon in the Secretary's room. Rev Rosslyn Bruce of Clifton, and Dr S. E. Gill, honorary Surgeon to the Class, had been specially invited by the Duchess. A footman then took Mr Clarke, Mr Bruce, Dr Gill and me into the front entrance where the Duchess received us, and led us into the dining room. I wish I could describe to you how beautiful Her Grace looked as she stood to welcome us so graciously — dressed in white, and so wonderfully sweet. On my way to the dining room Her Grace introduced me to her son, the Marquis of Tichfield (*sic*), just home from Eton (a boy of 14) and her daughter Lady Victoria Cavendish-Bentinck 2 years older than her brother. As our train was very late, the other guests had finished luncheon & had gone into the garden, so we four had the large dining room to ourselves. The Duchess sat by us and talked, and soon after we commenced our luncheon, the Duke came in and he sat and talked too, and was so very kind & nice. Just before we finished luncheon, the Duchess was called away, but before she left the room she said, "Will you come to me Miss Shaw when you have finished? You will find me in the Gothic Hall." I left the gentlemen alone with the Duke a few minutes later, and went as I thought towards the Gothic Hall. Of course I got lost, so I just waited, and soon I heard the sweet voice of Her Grace as she came to find me. And then I had the tremendous pleasure of being alone with the Duchess for about 20 minutes. As long as I live I shall never forget it. She took me to her bedroom and to her Boudoir, and I felt myself greatly honoured. I tried to thank her for the many kind things she had done for the Class and I told her how greatly we value her sympathy and help. Her Grace just looked at me with her wonderful eyes, and that smile which I am sure would melt the hardest heart, and she said how much she enjoyed hearing about the poor fellows, and their difficulties, and she told me to continue to write and tell her all about the Class — and she added some very kind words of sympathy and encouragement to me personally, and I was very very happy. You will I fear be disappointed that I do not describe the beautiful bedroom of Her Grace, and tell you about the many lovely things in her Boudoir, but I simply cannot. I just felt that I could not take my eyes from her face, and there were so many beautiful things in every room — but always, the most beautiful was the Duchess herself. Then we went into the Library where the four gentlemen joined us. The Duke pointed out many interesting objects in the Library and showed us some curious old manuscripts. Later on he took us into the private Chapel and explained how the present Chapel and Library had been made from the old Riding School, and he told us many interesting facts about both places.

We intended to make a little presentation to the Duchess immediately after the men had finished their luncheon, so we went from the Chapel to the Servant's Hall to find the men. I think we must have been longer in the Library than we thought, for when we arrived at the Servant's Hall, the men had gone with two guides to look at different parts of the Estate, and nobody seemed to know which way they had gone. The Duke said, "Never mind, Miss Shaw, we'll find them." So we returned to the Library for a few minutes to wait for two motor cars which His Grace ordered to take us to find the men. While we waited, I had another sweet little talk with the Duchess. She told me about her children, and that her eldest daughter, Lady Victoria, a girl of nearly 18 yrs, was coming out this autumn at the ball in November, when the King & Queen of Spain are coming to stay at Welbeck. How much I enjoyed watching the expression in the face of the Duchess when she spoke of her children. It is, I believe, because she is such a true woman that people love her so much. When the motor cars were ready, the Duchess left us, promising to meet us at tea time. The Duke, Mr Bruce and I got into one motor, Dr Gill and Mr Clarke into the other. But it took us quite 20 minutes to find the men. All the time, the Duke was so interesting and kind. He told Mr Bruce he ought to write a book entitled not "How we found Livingstone" but "How we found the 100 men we lost at Welbeck"! At last we saw the men, and you can imagine what ringing cheers they gave. The Duke told the men how pleased he was to see them — he hoped they would have a very good time. I can't describe to you how exceedingly kind he was. He took the men himself into the large Riding School and told them it was the second largest in the world. There is one larger at Moscow. At the time of Mr Chamberlain's visit, the Riding School held 12,000 people! Afterwards the Duke took the men to the Stables and we saw Simon Peter, the smallest pony in the world (a gift to the Duke's eldest son when he was a little boy). Then after admiring the horses very much, we were taken to the conservatories, and the lovely Orchid House etc.

Then the Duke said goodbye to us, and went to rejoin his other guests — but before he left, he shook hands with every man, and said some more kind things. My men did admire him — one man said, "Well I never thought a dook could be that free an' easy"!

During the half hour that remained before tea, the men went on to the lovely lawn in front of the house, where the fountains were playing and looking so pretty in the sunshine. They listened to the band and watched a cricket match. The Duke kindly called the Housekeeper and told her to show the ladies of our party (the six Sunday School helpers) some parts of the house. I went too, and we saw the State rooms, the drawing rooms, the Gothic Hall, and other beautiful rooms.

At 5.30 we all assembled in the Servant's Hall, and just before tea, the presentation took place. Let me explain about this. A few weeks after the Mikado party, one Sunday afternoon, after the Class, a large group of men stood talking together in rather a mysterious manner. One of them came up to me afterwards & said "I suppose, Miss Shaw, you know what we've been talking about." I sd. "No, indeed I do not." Then he said "Well you see it's like this, we all want to take the Duchess some'at when we go to Welbeck, so Fred Gough will be the Collector, and every Sunday we mean to give him a halfpenny each." Of course I was delighted, and the more so because the idea was entirely their own. The halfpennies at last amounted to £2. We wondered what to buy. One of the men said "Miss Shaw, why don't you write and ask the Duke what she would like?" I agreed to do so — told him the amount, and asked if he would kindly suggest to us some little thing the Duchess would really like. I also told him in my letter that some of the men had said "I wonder if we shall see the Dook when we go to Welbeck." His Grace kindly replied at once by telegram. It ran thus:— "Duchess most deeply touched. She would very much like a pencil case with little inscription. I shall be there. Portland." So we bought a gold pencil case, and on it were engraved these words "To Her Grace, the Duchess of Portland, with grateful love from the men in Miss Shaw's Class August 3rd 1907."

Now to return to the Servant's Hall. The men were all there when the Duchess went with me into the room. Of course they at once stood up and heartily clapped and cheered. How beautiful she looked as she smiled and bowed to the men, and their eyes gazed at her as though she were an angel as indeed I think she is. Then amid perfect silence, John Gill, one of the most faithful members of the Class, handed the gold pencil to the Duchess, and asked her to accept it from all the men, as a token of their love and gratitude. He thanked Her Grace for her many acts of kindness to the class, and said that on behalf of the men, he had a great favour to ask — it was this — would the Duchess kindly consent to become the President of our Class. John was rather nervous as he spoke, and once or twice his voice trembled so that I almost feared he would break down. He told me afterwards he had prayed many times, that he might be helped to do his part well.

Then Her Grace took the pencil and as she looked round on the faces of the poor men, some of them worn and thin from insufficient food, a sudden rush of crimson came to her face, and her voice for the first minute trembled more than John's had done and I am sure the tears were not far away. She quickly recovered her self control, and then she made the sweetest little speech to the men. She said, that as long as she lived, she would always keep and greatly value that pencil, and she told the men how pleased she was to see them at Welbeck, and how willingly she consented to be the President of the Class. How the men cheered when she said this! And how glad and thankful I was too! Her Grace put the pencil on her chain, and said to the men "Now doesn't that look nice?"

Then we all had tea. The Duchess went with me into the Secretary's room where tea was ready for the Sunday School Workers. She sat with us for a little time, and then said she would like to return to the Servant's Hall and talk to the men quite alone. How pleased the men were that she preferred being with them. They talked to her quite freely and naturally, and again and again, we in the Secretary's room, heard peals of laughter and hearty clapping from the Servant's Hall. One man said to me afterwards, speaking of the Duchess "She was that sweet we couldn't help talking to her." She wd. not come away till she had had a little talk with every man. When Her Grace left the men, she came to me and said, "Miss Shaw, I like your men very much indeed, they are most interesting. I have invited them all to come again next year, and told them in the meantime to double their numbers." Then indeed it was our turn to clap and rejoice.

We left Welbeck Abbey at 5.45 and I'm sure everyone was sorry when the Brakes arrived to take us to the Station. Her Grace shook hands with every man and said goodbye, and stood waving her hand to us till the last Brake had driven away amid loud cheering for the Duke & Duchess. Sometime, when we are talking together I should like to tell you some of the very droll remarks the men made about their visit to Welbeck. It was a wonderful day for all of us — a day that can never be forgotten. Later on the Duchess said in one of her letters, speaking of the men, "I simply loved having them, and enjoyed the afternoon quite as much as they did." And now she is our beloved President! God bless her.

It was the first of many happy visits, which were later alternated with Brackenhurst Hall near Southwell, the home of Sir William Hicking. The Marsden family would provide the comestibles for high tea from their shops and willing hands would prepare them. Mary Ellen records "cutting up" i.e. making sandwiches, herself, in the cricket pavilion at Brackenhust in 1916, and her thankfulness when Sir William gave her a cheque for £17, two days later, to cover all the expenses.

The Men's Bible Class was a great success; Mary Ellen was strict, but kind with the men and they respected her. She was known to patrol the pubs on pay day, seeking them out and sending them home with their wages. She was never afraid of venturing into unsavoury districts, either, sometimes accompanied by the family dog, armed only with her umbrella and a strong sense of what had to be done. She recommended a drawn hat-pin for defence in dark railway tunnels! And she *did* get results:

> It may be asked by some of my friends whether the Sunday afternoon Class is doing any definite good or making any difference in the lives of these men. May I tell you about a few of them.
>
> No.1 — A man who had such a vile character that I refused for some time to have him in the Class, lest he should contaminate the younger men — has now been five years without any intoxicating drink, and from being one of the dirtiest men in the Class has for 9 or 10 months come with clean hands & face & a white collar. The work is slow, but I am hopeful about him.
>
> No. 2 — A quiet miserable looking man, attended the Class 18 months and then he wrote to me these words "I am working with a lot of devils — I'm not a Christian but I'm trying to be one. Before I came to the Class, I was a Drunkard, a gambler, & a house breaker. Now I've chucked my bad companions. I luv the Class & I luv you."

She knew all the men by name and if any one of them fidgeted or fell asleep whilst she was talking, she would tap the lectern with her pencil and say sharply, "Frank (or whoever) — you're not listening!" Meetings always finished with a hymn and in time she published her own hymnal, *Selected Hymns for Miss Shaw's Bible Classes* containing such favourites as "Abide with me", "Count your blessings" and "God be with us till we meet again". Kalcie was sometimes enlisted to help teach them the hymn tunes line by line, as it was well-known that if they got it wrong the first time that version was likely to stick forever!

The Babies Guild

At some point in the early 1900s Mary Ellen became the Duchess's agent,[26] investigating the many claims for charitable assistance which emerged from the poor areas of the city. Mary Ellen knew these districts well and was able

[26] She was paid £25 per quarter plus expenses for this work in 1916.

to judge the needs of the people who struggled to survive in the dismal courts and alleys. She recalled entering one house where there was nothing on the table but half a broken plate with a small cube of lard on it and a few slices of bread; and in another house she found a woman trying to feed her baby with a pickled onion!

The answer to some of these problems was the setting up of a Mothers' and Babies' Welcome Guild in 1908 with the Duchess as President and Dr Gill as Medical Adviser. Women were taught the basics of hygiene and nutrition and how to care for their babies according to their means — for example, a cradle was not necessary for a new-born so long as a dresser drawer was available. Baby clothes and other basic equipment were lent out for a small fee; Mary Ellen believed poor people should be required to pay for things — if only a penny or two — because it allowed them to keep their self-respect and dignity. Each baby had a certificate signed by the Duchess and 'bonny baby' competitions were held to encourage the mothers to take care of their children. The Duchess herself would come to present the prizes — coveted push chairs, cribs and other luxuries not normally within the means of poor mothers.

A newspaper report under the headline, "Duchess of Portland Presents Prizes to Proud Nottingham Mothers"[27] described how she was welcomed by "a procession of tiny tots waving little Union Jacks above their heads ... each of these received a picture book at her Grace's hands." Here lay the secret of the Duchess's great popularity — her ability to make herself comfortable with all kinds and conditions of people and to actually enjoy herself. On that occasion she commented, "What I love most in Nottingham is the circle of friendly faces which always greet me here," and she certainly meant it. Welbeck Abbey was always available as a venue for days out and picnics for groups like these, and at Carburton, on the Welbeck Estate, the Duchess set up a sort of holiday cottage run by Nurse Annie Stenton, for ailing city children who would benefit from two or three weeks' fresh air and good food.

A child left orphaned or rescued from an abusive home would be carefully placed in suitable accommodation and Mary Ellen would make all the arrangements herself. In her 1916 diary she notes all that was involved in

27 *The Nottingham Daily Express*, Friday 17 March 1916

placing a seven-year-old girl called Lily Lindley whose father had been killed in an accident with a goods train on the Midland Railway and whose mother had recently died of cardiac disease. After collecting the child from Carburton, she took her to have her hair cut and put her to sleep in her own room at home before escorting her to Beddington Orphanage in Buckinghamshire, which she had previously inspected. She remained in touch with Lily, visiting her and sending her books etc. and years later even took her into service at Mansfield Road. There must have been many other children over the years whom she rescued from destitution.

Prison Visiting etc.

Other cases involved men and women — but especially women — who had become caught up irrevocably in crime and ended up in prison. Mary Ellen campaigned persistently until she was allowed into the Bagthorpe Prison and access to some of these sorry individuals. "Took female prisoner Mrs Rose to Mansfield," she writes on 12th Jan. 1916. "Gave her some lunch at Mikado Café first." One woman, whose confidence Mary Ellen gained, told her that when she could no longer stand her husband and domestic problems any longer, she would deliberately get drunk in order to go to prison "for a rest". She said it was, "like a holiday and gives me strength to go back to cope."

Drink was a problem as much for women as for men, as Mary Ellen knew only too well from Lucy's tragedy, often resorted to out of depression or despair. In her Quarterly Report to the Duchess in March 1912, she describes a case in point, brought to her attention through the Bible Class:

> Harold Swinton the young man who sang, "Oh that fog, that fearful fog" at our Mikado Supper, came to me 2 months ago & sd. he was in despair about his mother's drinking habits. Harold is the son of the man who was in penal servitude for 14 yrs. During the last 4 yrs, the Father, unable to get work, has been living on the earnings of his 3 good children & his wife. They grew tired of keeping him & the wife sd. a few "strong things". So he "took the hump" & went to London & they don't know where he is. The wife, who is really fond of him, fretted a good deal at his absence & gradually got into the fatal habit of taking spirits. She began to sell (secretly) little things from the home. Her two sons, both members of my Class, put up with much discomfort before telling me. Harold is a very shy young man, but at last one night after the

> Choir practise he walked up with me & told me all. He sd. "Miss Shaw, if it hadn't been for the Sunday Class, I shd. have left home altogether, but I thought of my sister & brother & felt I ought to stay." The next day I visited Mrs Swinton. I had not seen her for a yr. & she was greatly changed — dirty, untidy, and alas, on the table was a glass which had contained whiskey. She seemed pleased to see me and I tried to be very gentle with her to get to the actual truth. Gradually she told me everything. Then I spoke plainly & told her what an awful thing it wd. be to lose her comfortable little home & force the boys into early marriage. She cried bitterly & admitted everything. She sd. "I am just getting into an old degraded despised woman, & the man I love & have suffered so much for, has gone & left me, tho' I worked hard for the children all the yrs. he was in prison." So I told her that she was not despised or degraded — that only Drink cd. degrade & I begged her to give it up. Then I prayed with her. She sd. "Oh I will be different, I know I've been going the wrong way, but I've been so miserable." I asked her to go with me to the Sunday Evening Service. She sd. her clothes were not nice enough but she wd. think about it. A fortnight later Harold told me his mother was improving very much. I visited her again & last week Harold sd. "She's saving money to buy a new hat for Sunday Evening Service." I sd. "tell her I look for her every Sunday." Last Sunday night she & her daughter came. She wore a nice hat trimmed with black velvet & violets. As I passed her a hymn book I whispered "You do look nice" and she blushed with pleasure, & sang every word of the hymn. As we were leaving Harold managed to whisper "Doesn't Mother look different tonight" and I replied "She looks splendid, go on praying for her."

She ends this particular report:

> These little quarterly Reports only give a very faint idea of the work done. Much of it cannot be written. But more & more I feel that men & women can be saved & helped, & their lives made brighter ... One can only find out their real need by personal interviews & that is the reason I attach so much importance to regular & systematic visiting. Love and Prayer, & the Word of God are the means used, & are surely successful if only one is patient long enough.

And she thanks the Duchess for enabling her to continue with her work.

Support and Friendship

One wonders how Mary Ellen coped with all her different duties. By 1916 she was fifty-seven and no longer teaching but she was busier than ever. She still did district visiting — on 10th April she visited twenty homes in Carlton and Lenton, and on 25th, twenty-seven homes in Mansfield. Whenever she was tired out but had to get up and go to one more meeting, she famously used to say, "Lord, push me out!" A poem in her handwriting in the front of the Bible Class register for 1914 reads as follows:

We Two

"I cannot do it alone
The waves run fast and high
And the fogs close chill around
And light goes out in the sky
But I know that we two shall win
My God and I.

I could not row it myself
My boat on the raging sea
What of that? Another sits in my boat
And pulls or steers with me.
And I know that we two shall come safe into port
His child and He.

Coward, wayward and weak
I change with the changing sky
One day eager and brave
The next not caring to try
But He never gives in
And we two shall win
My God and I."

It may not be great poetry but it is deeply felt and provides the key to Mary Ellen's persistence and determination.

As always, she relied upon one or two friends to whom she went on a regular basis for meals and relaxation. At this period in her life those friends were Sir Arthur and Lady Black who lived at Springfield, Alexandra Park and the Leivers family at Clinton House, Sherwood Rise. She seems to have had supper with one or other family most days. The Richards family on Mapperley Road were also close; Mr Richards and his wife helped with the Bible Class and their daughter Ethel was to play a key role in it later on.

The two Withers families had now moved to Sidmouth where she continued to visit them. Mary was in poor health but always pleased to see her. Lillie Marshall and her two daughters also moved to Sidmouth in 1916 and Mary Ellen was on hand to make arrangements for them as they passed through Nottingham. Another long-time friend locally was a Mrs Emma Astill who often accompanied her to the Bible Classes in Mansfield, three in all, including two men's classes and one for woman by 1917.

But during this period, the support Mary Ellen probably valued most of all was that of "her" Duchess, who seemed to have the knack of knowing when she needed a short break and would invite her to stay at Welbeck as her guest for a few nights. During 1916 Mary Ellen stayed four times and records her pleasure in being pampered a little in gracious surroundings and her thankfulness for Her Grace's consideration. These stays were also business meetings — the Duchess examined Mary Ellen's accounts and discussed needy cases. The Bible Class registers were also checked and signed by the Duchess over the years, with little comments like, "Well done all of you!"

In a letter from Welbeck dated 24th April 1924, the Duchess wrote,

> The more I think of your class the more wonderful I feel it to be ... Take great care of yourself and do not get run down. Go away at once if you feel you are. Your life and work are much too precious to take any risks.
> Bless you, Yours sincerely,
> W. Portland.

Chapter 5: The War Years and beyond

Mary Ellen's endeavours were, of course, made more difficult by the War — Zeppelin raids, black-outs and petrol shortages made travel more difficult, though she seems not to have let such things interfere with her work.

> **Saturday 23rd September 1916:** Zeppelins. Did visiting in Old Basford. Rested and wrote letters in afternoon. After tea met Parker [one of the Bible Class men] at 5.30 & had tea at Mikado Café with him. Went to Springfield and to Clinton House to supper. At 9.35 the Buzzer went. I walked home in the darkness. We went to bed at 11.40 but at 12.40 were woken up by the noise of bombs dropping. We returned to bed at 2.15. Thank God for spared lives

Parker had probably just been called up. Mrs Astill was worried about her son Cyril being called up, and Jack Clarke had just had his call-up papers. Jack was to serve as a Lieutenant in the Royal Horse Artillery in Italy and Austria; but in the meantime he appeared regularly in musicals like "The Lily of Killarney", "Romance" and "Maritana" at the Grand Theatre and the Hippodrome. When not on stage, he and other members of his company entertained wounded soldiers at the General Hospital. Many men in the Bible Class were also called up. Registers surviving from this period for Nottingham and Mansfield show how Mary Ellen carefully recorded when they joined up, whether they were wounded or gassed, taken prisoner or killed in action. All were kept track of, written to, prayed for and the survivors welcomed home from the conflict. Her summary for 1915 reads, "135 men gone, 11 killed, 13 wounded, 6 making ammunition, 1 prisoner of war." Also in the margins she made notes of the possible needs of the men's families and tried to provide some comfort for them. Welbeck did what it could: consignments of rabbits shot on the estate were sent over, and potatoes, which would be distributed by a reliable member called Edgar to the other men of the Bible Class, ticking names off on a list so that each received something in turn.

The report of the men's annual dinner that year is particularly telling:

Miss Shaw's Bible Class[28]

Duchess of Portland Present at Annual gathering

> The Duchess of Portland and Lady Victoria Cavendish-Bentinck were present last evening at the annual gathering of the members of Miss Shaw's Bible Class, which is connected with the Mansfield-road Wesleyan Church, held at the Mikado Café, Nottingham. The preponderance of elderly men and youths was eloquent of the splendid patriotic record of the class. Of upwards of 400 members, no fewer than 172 have joined the forces, 28 were medically rejected, and six are munition workers. Of those who have served, 12 have been killed in action, one was taken prisoner and 25 have been wounded, one of whom (who was present) having been gassed and unconscious for three weeks, while another soldier wounded at Hooge was also able to attend.
>
> Captain J.A.H. Green presided at the gathering which followed the tea, being supported by her Grace and Lady Victoria Bentinck, the Rev. F. Hall and Mrs Hall, and Mr W.N. Hicking.
>
> In presenting 44 honour badges, the Duchess said that both the Duke and herself were pleased and proud at the record of the class.
>
> A cordial vote of thanks to the chairman and her Grace was passed on the proposition of Mr Hicking.
>
> A ventriloquist entertainment and Punch and Judy show were greatly enjoyed.

The honour badges were blue and white enamel lapel badges with the legend "Miss Shaw's Men's Bible Class" surrounding an open Bible on the front and a tiny portrait of the Duchess on the button at the back (see title page).

> Thus the men are encouraged to "go forth into the fight with sin and Satan, wearing their lady's favour on their breasts like knights of old."[29]

Numbers in the class dropped to around 180 during the War years, but in December 1918, Mary Ellen rallied her own troops once more and numbers rose again to 300.

Death of Herbert Clarke

Herbert died on 15th March 1921, aged sixty-two. He had only recently retired after thirty-eight years as Registrar of births, marriages and deaths.

---

28 *The Nottingham Daily Express*, Friday 10 March 1916.

29 John Gould in the *Methodist Recorder*, 7 March 1912.

During his time in office, the population of his area of North East Nottingham had increased three-fold to around 65,000 and the increasing workload had taken its toll on his health. The house at 86 Mansfield Road had been a registrar's office for forty-eight years and this time there was no family member to take over. Herbert's estate was worth nearly £10,000 — he owned 86 Mansfield Road and 84 next door, as well as thirteen other leasehold properties and a half-share in freehold land on Carlton Hill.[30] That being the case, his legacy of £200 to Mary Ellen seems unnecessarily meagre. She was now sixty-two with no independent means of support and had lived and worked in his household for twenty-five years. However, Herbert *had* provided for his daughters, having invested £1000 each for them, and stated they were to have the use of the furniture etc. at 86 for as long as they remained unmarried. This must have meant the house as well and it was assumed that Mary Ellen would continue to live with them. Kalcie (Kathleen) married Herbert Synyer the following year, but Nora was never to marry and continued to need the assistance of her Aunt, so they remained there together. Mary Ellen was still living there in 1925, and a Servant's Registry run by a Miss Hulme (possibly Miss N. Hulme, her co-worker — see page 53) is operating from the same address, so unused space was probably rented out. By 1926, the year of Mary Ellen's death, Charles H. Truman was Registrar and using the office, but he lived in West Bridgford.

Samborne Cook had long been at the forefront of public life in Nottingham, not only as a successful businessman, but as a J.P., a Liberal Councillor and, in 1905, Sheriff , an office "which he discharged with the greatest credit to himself."[31] However, his health was not good and he turned down the opportunity to become Mayor. He and Maud moved to Bournemouth in 1915, leaving nephew Herbert Clarke in charge of the business. Maud returned to run stall 47a with her daughter Gladys Wade at the great Patriotic Fair put on to boost morale and local trade by the Portlands in May 1917 — selling Toilet Soaps! On Sam's death on 26th July 1926, Bertie became sole proprietor of the business. Maud eventually returned to Nottingham and lived in Calstock Road, Woodthorpe, with her

---

30 Notts. Archives ref. DD2553/15-17

31 *The Trader*, Nottingham, 12 February 1909.

daughter Florence until her death on 20th October 1948, at the age of eighty-seven.

Mary Ellen must have been quite lonely at Mansfield Road with only Nora for company. She and Herbert had jogged along quite comfortably together and he had involved himself with the Bible Class in many helpful ways, such as organising the annual trips and providing entertainment at the dinners. Mary Ellen respected him and all he stood for as her father's successor and when she believed the General Register Office had served him badly in his retirement, she leapt to his defence. All Registrars had been granted a bonus of £50 for extra work done during the War, but because Herbert had just retired he did not receive it, which Mary Ellen considered grossly unfair. In a letter to the GRO on 31st March 1921 she told them so, in no uncertain terms, stating that, "He was a man who loved peace and hated friction or quarrelling — hence he would not even speak about the injustice." She also made the slightly bizarre request that she be allowed to keep the small iron safe which had stood in the house since her Father's time, and it is still in the family.

Death of Mary Ellen Shaw

Mary Ellen died on Christmas Eve 1926, at the Central Nursing Home, 18 Regent Street, after surgery for breast cancer complicated by thrombosis. Perhaps she suspected that she was coming to the end of her journey but she faced it with characteristic courage and strength drawn from an unshakeable faith. The night before she entered the nursing home she wrote out this verse by Victor Hugo:

Sleep sweetly in this quiet room
O thou who'ere thou art,
And let no mournful yesterdays
Disturb thy quiet heart,
Nor let tomorrow scare thy rest
With dreams of coming ill,
Thy Master is thy changeless friend,
His love surrounds thee still.
Forget thyself and all the world,
Put out each glaring light,

The stars are watching overhead,
Sleep sweetly then,
Good-night.

Her modest estate was handled by her niece Kathleen and friend Mrs Ellen Richards. Typical of her, of only two personal bequests, she left £50 to the child Lily Lindley, who, when the will was made in 1921, was back in Nottingham, living in the Midland Orphanage, Lenton.

On 29th December the *Nottingham Journal* described her funeral, an event worthy of the impact she had made on many lives. Three clergymen officiated, the Duke of Portland himself attended and the church was packed:

The Funeral of Miss E. Shaw

Striking Nottingham Tributes

Striking tributes of friendship and respect were witnessed at the funeral in Nottingham yesterday of Miss E. Shaw, well-known in the city as leader for many years of a large men's Bible class at Mansfield-road Wesleyan Church.

Her devoted religious work included the conducting of men's and women's classes at the Mansfield-road church and at Mansfield; and members of these numbering several hundreds followed the coffin (after a service in the Mansfield-road church) to the Church Cemetery, where the interment took place.

A Noble Life

The Duke of Portland, who shared the direct interest which the Duchess took in Miss Shaw's work, was present and brought a wreath.

The Rev. J. Freeman made eloquent references to Miss Shaw's life and work at the pre-interment service, which was conducted by the Rev. P. I. Watchurst, and at which the congregation filled the church. "She has accomplished a work," he said, "of which not only the church but the city may well be proud." Before the war her Nottingham men's class had nearly 500 members, and today it had over 300.

Addressing the members present, Mr Freeman made the appeal: "You won't let her down? You won't forsake the class and the work?" and there was a chorus of "No!" in response.

Numerous Wreaths

The Rev. F. J. Pratt officiated at the interment. The private mourners were Miss Nora Clarke (niece), Mr John Clarke (nephew), Mrs H. Synyer (niece), Mr H. Renshaw Clarke (nephew), Mr and Mrs A. Richards, and Miss Hulme. There were also present Sir William Hicking, Mr W. G. Player, Mrs Frank Seely, Mr Hedley Fisher (representing Mr J. D. Marsden), Mrs J. A. Dixon, Mrs Clifton (Clifton Hall), Mr H. G. Supple (governor of Nottingham Gaol), the Rev. D. Selby (chaplain of the gaol), Ald. E. L. & Mrs Manning, the Rev. J. G. Thornton, Mr H. G. Thornton. Dr Cole, Dr Everard (Mansfield), Mr J. W. Hulme, Mr W. & Mrs Cost and Mrs Eking. Among numerous wreaths were floral tributes from the Nottingham and Mansfield classes.

"Her life was service"

The church was packed once again on November 5th 1927 when a Memorial Service was held. The reporter from the *Methodist Recorder*[32] said he had never attended a service quite like it; the Duke's own Chaplain read the lesson and Her Grace the Duchess of Portland unveiled a memorial tablet, paid for by members of the Bible classes.[33]

The Rev. John Freeman spoke of Mary Ellen's vision:

> Her heart yearned especially for those who had suffered through misfortune, and whose lives were drab. It was always characteristic of her that she immediately translated her vision into action...
>
> Nothing was left to chance. Everything was carefully thought out and planned. Her addresses to the men were written out and typed. She gave the men of her best. Once she gave a series of forty addresses on the life of Joseph, and then the men wanted more. Her activities were not confined to such work. She had a big heart, and always acted on her generous impulses, so got things done while others were dreaming... She will always be remembered as a great and successful worker for men, of whom this city may be justly proud.

All the men were presented with a framed photograph of Miss Shaw by the Duchess, a special gift from the Duke. Printed on the back of the photos was the tribute, "Her name liveth for evermore," conferring upon her the dignity

---

32 "H.M.", *Methodist Recorder* 10 November 1927.

33 This memorial was sadly lost after the congregation moved in 1940.

of a fallen soldier. The service finished with the familiar hymn, "God be with you till we meet again".

The following Sunday the reporter attended a meeting of the Nottingham Class and wrote:

> The area of the lofty Church was well filled, and many, including a large number of young men, sat in the galleries. Some men limped in on crutches; I saw at least one who was blind, led to his seat. As they came in, from a back entrance to the Church, the members handed their cards to the registrars, and nearly all were personally welcomed by Mr Richards. There was a good deal of brotherly handshaking. Again I noticed that some of the men looked very poor; some of the older ones had faces that told their own story of deprivation, illness, and struggle; one or two held their hymn-books with trembling hands... I was interested in the special hymn-book which Miss Shaw compiled for them, and which contained simple, popular choruses, such as, "I never could do without Jesus." One felt as the men sang that the words—
>
> > O many a time I am weary,
> > And many a time I am tired,
>
> represented a familiar experience of many there. Mr Richards, who is a quiet, unassuming man with a face that is glowing with earnestness and benevolence, conducted the meeting, which only occupied one hour. These men are wonderful listeners. They strain their ears to catch every word. So far as the addresses are concerned, my impression is that the strength of the Class has never been due so much to what has been *said* as to what has been *done*. These are men who appreciate the practical Christianity that resolves itself into fellowship and service, that follows them into the home and into the hospital, helping them to their last hour. This is really "living Methodism."
>
> As I came down from the pulpit, from which I had looked into the faces — (some, very pathetic, patient faces) — of the men, with some vague understanding of what the love of people like Miss Shaw and Mr Richards means to them, I glanced again at the memorial tablet. This was part of the simple inscription—

"Her life was service, and her service was love."

Epilogue

Mary Ellen had many devoted helpers in her work with the Bible Class and it continued to flourish after her death. Mrs Crumpton had been her faithful co-worker; and Miss N. Hulme, who had acted as her Secretary and helped with the visiting, carried on with the Women's Class under her married name of Skinner for some years. Mr Arthur Richards, an old friend and helper took over the leadership until 1935, to be succeeded by Mr Ernest Maule until his death, and then Mr Edward Dales until he died in 1961. The Mansfield Men's Class was served by Mr and Mrs Sidebotham and later by Mr and Mrs Urquart.

The Duchess remained their much-loved President and continued to attend their annual Mikado dinner and welcome the men to Welbeck. Three years after Mary Ellen's death 250 men attended the 1930 dinner which was chaired by Lieut.-Col. P.R. Clifton, High Sheriff of Nottinghamshire, who remarked that:

> It did him a world of good to see such a large gathering. There had been a great deal of talk about class distinction, but in such a gathering as that there was nothing in it. They were all flesh and blood, and brothers and sisters. [...] It was the spirit of brotherhood and fellowship, such as was engendered by Miss Shaw's Bible Class, that was needed. That night they remembered all she did and hoped that her work would always live. [34]

The Wesleyans left the Chapel on the corner of Woodborough Road in 1940 and moved in with the congregation at Redcliffe Road. The Men's Bible Class in Nottingham dwindled gradually over the years, their final meeting place being the Little Church on Bluecoat Street. It was Miss Ethel Richards, daughter of Ellen and Arthur Richards and a former headmistress of Nottingham Girl's High School kindergarten, who faithfully cared for the remnant, and the detailed notes she made for newspaper articles and addresses to mark anniversaries and keep the memory of Mary Ellen alive have been most helpful.

---

[34] *The Nottingham Guardian* 18 March 1930.

Myra Chilvers, Mary Ellen's great-niece, helped Miss Richards towards the end. She recalls, "Those few still generated a wonderful spiritual atmosphere and fellowship which quickly wrapped round me on my first visit when Miss Richard introduced me as Miss Shaw's niece."

The final meeting of Miss Shaw's Men's Bible Class took place on Sunday 30th August 1964.

Index

Note: women are listed by both married and maiden names as they appear in the text. If they are shown with a née it is worth also searching under their previous surname.

Also in this series:

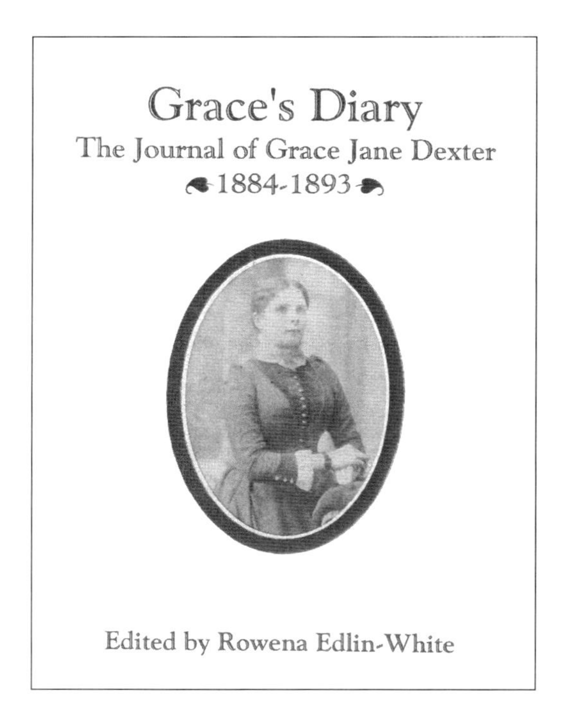

The diary of a young teacher in Nottingham, Derbyshire and London's East End in the closing years of the 19th century. Grace Dexter (1865-1963) was inspired and encouragedfor the whole of her long life by her friendship with Florence Nightingale. ISBN 1-900074-16-8